Leadership
Succession

Stewart D. Friedman

With a new introduction by the author

Transaction Publishers
New Brunswick (U.S.A.) and London (U.K.)

Library of Congress Catalog Number: 2011000831
ISBN 978-1-4128-4236-5
Printed in the United States of America

Library of Congress Cataloging-in-Publication Data

Leadership succession / [edited by] Stewart D. Friedman.
    p. cm.
    ISBN 978-1-4128-4236-5 (pbk.)
    1. Executive succession--United States. 2. Leadership--United States. I. Friedman, Stewart D.

HD38.25.U6L43 2011
658.4'0711--dc22
                                                    2011000831

CONTENTS

Introduction to the Paperback Edition of *Leadership Succession*

Stewart D. Friedman

In the 25 years that have passed since the first publication of this book, the landscape of leadership has been radically re-shaped, yet many of the ideas and challenges addressed in its pages seem to me to be as relevant as ever.

The academic literature is less consumed today than it was then with the question of whether or not leaders matter in affecting organization outcomes. Since the 1980s there has been much attention paid to re-searching the conditions under which different kinds of leaders—and the manner of their selection and development—matter. In the 1990s, theories of emotional and social intelligence emerged as researchers sought models of leadership that encompassed the personal: Leader-ship studies began to focus on the person within the leader and the value of connecting with the basic humanity of others. And in the past decade, there is an increasing emphasis on sustainability—of our personal, social, and natural resources—and so the focus of scholars of leadership has shifted thus.

Leadership was and is about mobilizing resources toward achiev-ing valued goals, but so much about it has changed. For one thing, leadership is no longer thought of as being just about people at the top of the pyramid; it is widely viewed as an attribute that anyone, at any level, can develop. And it's now commonly understood that to be successful, organizations must systematically invest in the cultivation of future leaders.

Here are some of the other changes in the context of leadership that I observed in my 2008 book, *Total Leadership*, which focuses on leader-ship from the point of view of the whole person:

> The single-earner father and stay-at-home mother have been replaced by diverse models of "the stan-dard home," demanding a radical revision in the expectations for time devoted to work, by men and women. Gender equity, while not yet achieved, is

gaining ground in all spheres of society, creating new expectations and opportunities. In the wake of recent corporate scandals, the status of business is low and citizens demand greater corporate accountability and ethical action. New public policies oblige business executives to find firmer moral ground and to avoid the temptations of greed.

People want to do work that has a positive impact on a world in which conflict seems pervasive. The best companies to work for are those in which employees work hard while having fun with people they see as their friends. Yet loyalty to a single organization (the model of my youth) is gone.

The digital revolution is forcing everyone to learn how to exploit new communication tools that promise freedom (allowing us not to be bound to a particular time or place), but often lead to a new kind of slavery (24/7 connectivity). New media require that we—as leaders of our lives—choose where, when and how to get things done, to manage the boundaries between different parts of life. This sets us apart from all prior generations, whose work routines were determined by the turning of the seasons and the rising and setting of the sun.

The torrid pace of change is compelling everyone in business to adapt to new situations, all the time. Ever-increasing demand for better productivity stresses and fragments our lives, causing health problems and burnout. At the same time, businesses are competing in the "war for talent" as labor shortages continue in critical sectors of the economy. Flatter organization structures mean a greater sense of responsibility for all, while globalization and the increasingly diverse pool of employees require new approaches to motivating people from different backgrounds.

With all these societal, technological, political and economic shifts, the timeless questions of how to prepare the next generation and choose among them remain vexing. Bob Dylan warned his elders, in 1964, "Your old road is rapidly aging. Please get out of the new one if you can't lend your hand." Am I standing in the way or offering a hand to those coming after me? I wonder how you, dear reader, would answer this question. Recent experiences have left me thinking often of that now-iconic line.

This past year, for example, I had the chance to hear Bill Clinton give a commencement speech to my eldest child and his classmates; I ran a half-day session on leadership with ten General Electric (GE) company officers, followed by dinner with CEO Jeff Immelt; and I led a meeting with the dozen or so physicians who constitute the senior executive corps of the University of Pennsylvania School of Medicine.

As hard as it might be for old folks in positions of power to see the world in a new light and embrace it, these senior people—and others, with whom I've been working—are trying their best to lend a hand to the next generation as they roll down a new road. Smart seniors who want to leave a positive legacy will pay attention to these and other examples, learn from them, and follow suit in a way that works in their world.

For decades GE has been, and remains, the most prolific net exporter of leadership talent in the corporate world, because it has a tradition—a strongly held cultural belief—supported by the tangible commitment of time and money, for developing people. You need not look any further than my recent visit to GE's corporate headquarters for some evidence. The expressed intent of my visit was to stimulate dialogue and raise provocative questions about what leadership means today and what it should mean in the future. With the full backing, even prodding, I felt from Chief Learning Officer Susan Peters, I encountered a readiness to challenge the status quo—to look at leadership from the perspective of not just work, but of the whole person, including family and community and personal life (mind, body, and spirit)—that was as refreshing as it was inspiring. Taking time "to address the soul," as one attendee put it, is not how things would've been done at GE back in the day; but, in 2010, knowing that the world has evolved and that a new leadership model is necessary for the people who will run GE in 2020, the current executives of this visionary company are taking important steps to critically evaluate, and so revise, their approach.

The University of Pennsylvania's School of Medicine is the site of an NIH-funded study of the impact of a series of interventions—including, full disclosure, my Total Leadership program—on the careers and lives of talented up-and-coming women faculty in academic medicine. This first-of-its kind project is an extension of remarkable efforts led by the FOCUS program, a unique initiative dedicated to advancing the careers of women faculty. Our meeting was a briefing for the top team on what we are undertaking, and why. Here, in one of the most tradition-bound fields, senior executives were engaging actively in a practical discussion about the nitty-gritty of what it would take to provide support for the next generation to succeed in experimenting with new ways to lead and get things done that are in synch with the demands of their lives beyond work; to do nothing less than re-think the culture of academic medicine.

President Clinton aimed one of his rhetorical arrows at this same target: To his audience of fresh-faced grads he declared that you, the rising generation, must focus on devising new ways to live and work that fit with the needs and interests not only of your work and your families, but of your spirit, of our society, and of our intricately interconnected world.

Tomorrow's leaders need all the help we can give them. Fortunately, there are some wise men and women who know this and are dedicating serious effort to exploring innovative ways to prepare them and to choose them. I have seen and heard them first-hand struggling to figure out a way forward on the new road. My impressions lead me to be optimistic, despite the enormous resistance inherent in the status quo and the difficulties of successfully inventing new forms of organization that will work better than those we have now. My hope is that the articles in this collection will be of some use in this noble effort.

Prologue

Stewart D. Friedman

Leadership succession—the matter of who shall rule [to quote Zald's (1965) telling title]—has been the subject of scholarly and popular attention since Plato expounded on the succession of philosopher-kings in his *Republic*. Why then a special issue of *Human Resource Management* now? Because this ubiquitous phenomenon is currently of particularly pressing practical, theoretical, and societal import.

The need for practical knowledge about leadership succession is urgent today because of the emerging recognition of human assets as critical in the effective implementation of business strategy. With the field of human resource management becoming more sophisticated and influential, the human resource function in organizations is better able to address significant questions bearing on business strategy. Contrary to general opinion as recent as a decade ago, it is now widely accepted that in order to meet the demands of a complex, turbulent environment, organizations must have effective human resource strategies. The authors in this issue speak directly to the human resource–business strategy linkage as a matter of practical importance in managing leadership succession.

In the world of management practice the succession problem is omnipresent, even if implicitly. In all organizations the challenges and opportunities inherent in the need to replace current executives is continuous, for leaders are mortal. The question is how to manage the succession process in a way that yields optimal outcomes for both the individuals involved and the organizations in which they work. The articles in this special issue aim to shed light on how best to manage the selection and development of present and future leaders.

In the world of theory, the field of organization sciences continues to seek a definitive answer to the fundamental question "Do leaders matter?" Two leading theories, strategic choice and population ecology, represent polar extremes on this issue. The former posits that leaders do indeed influence the fortunes of organizations, the latter that the survival of organizations is the result of forces beyond the control of their members. The current (and apparently growing) fascination with leadership succession in the literature of organization sciences (as seen, for example, in the 1985 program of the Academy of Management) is due to the opportunity to test competing hypotheses about succession and its effects that derive from different theories. For instance, if it can be shown that a change in leadership determines a predictable change in organizational performance, then one can conclude that leaders do matter; that the role of chief executive is not merely a symbolic one.

One of the potential contributions of this issue of *Human Resource Management* is to provide fresh ideas about the moderating influence of situational contexts in determining whether or not changes in leadership affect organizational outcomes. Leadership succession is viewed here as a means by which organizations adapt to changing environmental contexts, as a kind of organizational renewal. With change in the incumbency of a leadership position comes a new view of how to enact the role.

Theoretically, a distinction can be made between succession *events* and the succession *process*. The process pertains to how the critical decisions are made (e.g., who is involved, whence information comes, how much time is spent), in contrast to the outcome of the event (i.e., which new person moves into which position). Research on succession should investigate process variables because they influence whether succession event outcomes are seen as equitable. That is, the nature of the process—whether democratic, meritocratic, or oligarchic—will likely affect morale and perceptions of legitimacy of the governance structure in organizations. Most previous research has focused on events; another objective of this special issue is to address the process and the contextual conditions surrounding succession events.

In addition to the practical and theoretical importance of the subject, there is the glamour and gossip attending the succession of leaders that compels society's interest. At root the matter is political. And the stakes are high. Indeed, one of the reasons why there has been a paucity of empirical studies of succession processes is that it is difficult to obtain valid data on such politically hot topics. Our society appears to hold a fascination with celebrity. Some of today's organizational leaders are folk heroes; myths about them permeate our culture as never before. Various popular media are flooded with stories of the rise and fall of corporate executives and entrepreneurs (two of whose books are reviewed in this issue). Popular interest in leadership in general, and in leadership succession in specific is, therefore, another reason for this issue.

The order in which the articles appear reflects the differences among them in level of analysis. The first three (by Friedman, Gupta, and Hall) are about succession systems—the rules and procedures that form the context for the *typical* succession event (i.e., change in job incumbency) in the managerial ranks, including executive development and recruitment practices—not CEO succession per se. Then Bowman, Lundberg, and Sonnenfeld primarily address succession and related concerns at the CEO level, including the dynamic contexts of CEO succession events and the tensions that exist in the act of passing the torch. The last article, by Cowherd, is a view from the outside: an interview with the head of the world's largest executive recruiting firm on succession systems and CEO succession. We conclude with two reviews, one by Hornstein and the other by Singh, of books by CEOs.

The first article is a presentation of my study of succession systems in 235 large corporations. I describe succession systems for the top echelons (i.e., three levels below CEO) of these firms using a seven-dimensional framework. I address the "does it matter?" question by testing for differences between high and low performing firms (assessed with financial and reputation data) in succession system characteristics and conclude with a set of implications for managing succession systems.

Next is Gupta's article on matching managers to strategies. He has written influential papers on how this matter is handled at the strategic business unit (SBU) level. Here he takes a critical look at the pros and cons of this central succession system issue. He argues that matching people to positions may not always be appropriate. His ideas deepen our understanding of the conditions under which succession as strategic adaptation, the fitting of person with position given environmental demands, can and cannot occur.

Where Gupta's piece addresses selection and placement issues, Hall's focuses on executive development as part and parcel of succession systems. After describing the evolutionary patterns of succession systems, he argues for greater attention to executive learning in creating the highquality pools of management talent that are, he avers, necessary for effective succession systems. He concludes with a comprehensive set of recommendations for how this can be accomplished.

Bowman's article begins the second "chapter" of this special issue with his study of CEO concerns. He presents the results of his extensive interviews with a variety of CEOs. Perhaps most striking in his descriptive findings is the salience of management development and succession-related dilemmas in the minds of CEOs. After viewing the concerns of the CEO through four distinct conceptual lenses, he concludes that CEO concerns are best elucidated in terms of different levels of strategy and that CEO's direct their attention to internal matters more than is commonly thought.

Lundberg's essay offers a set of frameworks for analyzing the variety of organizational contexts in which chief executive succession occurs. In particular, he discusses the implications of stages in organizational life cycles—and how they are passed through—for executive succession processes. The roles that CEOs are expected to play in different contexts and at different stages should influence, he argues, the selection criteria applied in the choice among candidates as well as the kinds of developmental experiences needed for the growth of future CEOs.

Sonnenfeld's article is a call for attention to an heretofore neglected, yet critical and poignant, aspect of succession: departing leaders and the manner of their partings. Based on his extensive field research, he takes the position that departures are significant and tense events not only for those who are retiring, but also for those who are taking over and for others in the departing leader's constituency. He posits that smooth transitions are desirable for all concerned, especially for the community represented and personified by the one who is passing on. This unique perspective increases our awareness of the breadth and depth of the ramifications of chief executive succession events and processes.

The closing piece is Cowherd's engaging interview with Lester Korn, Chairman and CEO of Korn/Ferry International, the executive recruiting firm. After introducing the dialogue by way of an historical overview of the executive search industry and Korn/Ferry's role in it, Cowherd inquires about Korn's views on succession systems, executive search processes, roles of both boards of directors and of internal human resource professionals, and the future of the recruiting industry.

The issue closes with reviews of two books written by CEOs, one current, one retired. The first review, by Hornstein, is an insightful examination of *Iacocca: An Autobiography* that speaks to the urgency of leaders, incoming and departing ones, having courage—a quality this leader seems to manifest—for creating and sustaining organizational vitality. The second is a review by Singh of Harold Geneen's *Managing*. He takes a critical look at Geneen's philosophy and practice of management, focusing on the paradoxes in his leadership style and their long-term implications for large conglomerates like ITT.

Leadership succession is a matter of timely relevance and substantial consequence. The need to be concerned about the challenges facing today's leaders may be obvious; but to prepare tomorrow's leaders and to select them well is, to quote Coleridge, "common sense in an uncommon degree." Forward-thinking American Indian tribes made major decisions contingent upon the effects of the decisions on seven generations hence. Perhaps such foresight is not possible in the tumultuous world of contemporary organizations. Still, it is hoped that in the contents of this special issue the reader will find new and useful ideas about the passing on of legitimate power in our modern tribes.

REFERENCE

Zald, M. N. Who shall rule? A political analysis of succession in a large welfare organization. *Pacific Sociological Review*, 1965, **8,** 52–60.

Succession Systems in Large Corporations: Characteristics and Correlates of Performance*

— Stewart D. Friedman —

In this article succession systems in large corporations are characterized in terms of seven dimensions: formalization, control systems, resource allocation, information systems, political criteria, technical criteria, and staff role. Descriptive data drawn from a survey of key informants in 235 firms are presented. Hypothesized relationships between succession system characteristics and organization-level performance measures (corporate reputation and financial performance), given the effects of contextual conditions, are tested. Results reveal that high and low performing firms differ with respect to how they manifest succession systems. Six implications for how succession systems should be managed are proposed.

INTRODUCTION

How are the leaders of large corporations developed and selected for their positions? Is there a relationship between these features of organizational activity and organizational performance? The literature on leadership succession and its relationship to organizational performance is advancing from its early focus on just the antecedents and consequences of leadership succession events. Recent investigations have honed in on the moderating influences of both the organizational and environmental contexts in which succession events occur (e.g., Carroll, 1984; House et al., 1985; Lundberg, 1986; and Tushman et al., 1985) as well as on the characteristics of the individuals involved (other than whether or not successors come from within) (e.g., Gupta, 1984; Hambrick and Finkelstein, forthcoming 1987; Pfeffer and Davis-Blake, 1986; and Smith et al., 1984). Nonetheless, there has been little attention devoted either to the process by which succession events occur or to the management practices affecting the process and its outcomes in spite of the calls for such investigations by previous researchers (e.g., Lieberson and O'Connor, 1972: 128; Zald, 1970).

* The author gratefully acknowledges the following people for their advice and comments on this article: Hallie Friedman, David Brussard, Anil Gupta, Douglas T. Hall, Paul Olk, Len Rico, Greg Shea, Noel Tichy, and Carole Barnett.

This article reports the major findings of a study of these issues in 235 Fortune Industrial and Service 500 firms. It is an attempt to add to the succession literature by explicitly examining succession *systems*, rather than the mere *event* of leadership succession, and how these systems can and do relate to important organization-level outcomes, given the effects of contextual conditions.

A set of definitions and a research model of the critical aspects of succession systems and how they bear on the performance of large corporations are outlined. Next, the sample and methods are reviewed. Then, selected descriptive results are presented to address the question, "What do the succession systems of these firms look like?" The following section indicates which characteristics of succession systems do indeed correlate significantly with a set of organizational performance measures. Based on these relationships, six implications are proposed for how succession systems should be managed.

DEFINITIONS AND RESEARCH MODEL

Succession systems are defined as the rules and procedures that form the context for a typical succession event (i.e., a change in job incumbency), including executive development and placement practices. It is assumed that all organizations have succession systems. They are ubiquitous; all organizations face the challenges and opportunities inherent in the need to replace current leaders. Just as all organizations are culture-bearing (Louis, 1983), so too are they all media for power struggles. The question is, how are these matters managed? What are the principles and practices that guide this essentially political (Pfeffer and Salancik, 1978; Zald, 1970) process? This study focuses on succession systems for the top echelon of large corporations, defined as the top three levels below the CEO in the management hierarchy. CEO succession, because it is an idiosyncratic and relatively rare event, is not considered here. Rather, our interest is in examining how succession events typically unfold throughout the top echelon and in the management practices that critically affect these events.

The *succession process*—the means by which succession decisions are made—is described in a four-stage model. The stages represent decisions about: (1) establishing the need for a succession event, (2) determining selection criteria, (3) selecting candidates, and (4) choosing among the candidates. This model implies rationality in the succession process; that individuals are selected because they fit best with position requirements. Certainly this is not always the case. One can easily imagine, for example, succession events in which the last stage, choice of candidate, occurs first; the prior stages are then explained by key decision-makers in a way that provides a rationale for the choice. The model does, however, provide a framework for analyzing the salient features of any succession event. A detailed analysis would inquire about each of the four stages of the decision process: (a) who is involved, (b) reasons for the decision, (c) procedures for coming to it, (d) the time span over which it was made, (e) sources of information tapped, and (f) the amount of effort, time, and energy explained in the decision process during that stage.

The research model that guides this investigation is presented in Figure 1. Three sets of variables are measured: succession system characteristics, contextual conditions, and organization-level outcomes. In order to simplify the task of describing succession system characteristics, the first research objective, seven dimensions were derived from a series of pilot investigations (Friedman, 1984). Definitions and selected findings for each dimension are presented in the next section.

The second research objective is to assess whether or not, and to what extent, succession system characteristics are related to organizational performance outcomes. Does it matter how leaders are developed and selected for their positions of power? The basic hypothesis is that a firm will have a good reputation and will perform well financially, compared to other firms, if it has a succession system, again relative to others, that

- is highly formalized,
- has a system of checks and balances,
- has sufficient resources allocated to it,
- has extensive and comprehensive information on people and positions,
- uses criteria for selection decisions based on technical competence and not on political ties, and
- has staff people who are credible but who do not "own" the system.

In other words, such a system will result in the appropriate development and placement of people for positions of leadership. Good use is made of a firm's human assets if there is systematic evaluation of people and positions and a succession process that allows for their appropriate match. If people are developed and placed well, then they, and the organizations in which they work, should perform well too. Arrow 1 in Figure 1 connotes this basic relationship.

To empirically assess this hypothesis, critical outcomes as well as contextual conditions are measured. The relevant outcomes are corporate reputation, financial performance, turnover in the management ranks, and the perceived (by a key informant from each organization) effectiveness of the succession system. In this article only the first two are considered. Corporate reputation data, available for a subset of the sample only (explained below in "Methods and Sample"), are taken from the first two years of *Fortune's* annual survey of corporate reputation (Makin, 1983; Perry, 1984), which measures eight dimensions of reputation. Two are of particular interest: the ability to attract, develop,

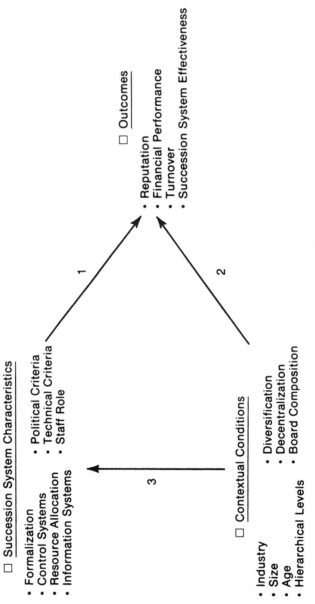

Figure 1. The research model: succession systems, contextual conditions, and outcomes.

and retain talented employees and the firm's reputed quality of management. Financial performance is measured five different ways: four return ratios (on sales, equity, total assets, and total invested capital) and stock appreciation plus dividends per share. All five are annual averages taken over the five year period up to the year prior to when the succession systems were measured (early 1984).

The third set of variables are contextual conditions. Arrow 2 in Figure 1 suggests that these seven aspects of an organization's context will affect the outcomes at interest. They are included in this study in order to control for their effects in examining the Arrow 1 relationships. That is, over and above the effects of contextual conditions, do succession system characteristics relate to the outcomes?

Arrow 3 concerns how context affects succession systems. Under what conditions do succession systems vary? For instance, do diversified firms have more extensive and powerful staff roles than single-line businesses? One might expect this to be true given the need for greater coordination at the corporate level in diversified firms. However, the relationships implied by Arrow 3 are not discussed in detail in this article (see Friedman, 1984 for analyses of these relationships). To reiterate, contextual conditions are noted here solely because they are taken into account when examining the associations between succession systems and outcomes.

METHODS AND SAMPLE

The Leadership Succession Survey

Table I outlines the topics covered in the 26-page questionnaire that was administered by mail to a representative of each organization in the 1984 Fortune Industrial and Service 500 listings; the population included 1000 firms. The first section asks about background and context, including number of hierarchical levels, extent of diversification, etc. The second section asks about succession systems for the top echelon. The third section is about the succession of the former to the current CEO. (Data from this last section are not analyzed in this article.)

Choice of Sample and Response Rate

This population was selected for three reasons. First, much of the previous research on succession practices focuses on the population of U.S. corporations, with some variation in size of firms (e.g., Fulmer, 1978; Lieberson and O'Connor, 1972; Shaeffer, 1982; Weiner, 1977). Comparability with previous research, then, was a critical factor in sample choice. Second, all the firms in the sample are publicly held. Their

Table I.   Measuring Succession System Characteristics: Content of the Leadership Succession Survey.

Background
- Respondent's role and responsibilities
- Number of CEOs in company's history
- Reports to CEO
- Existence of succession planning staff function
- Number of hierarchical levels
- Types of organization structure
- Lines of business
- Economic growth stage of company
- Number of employees
- Rates of turnover

Succession Systems for the Top Echelon
- Replacement plans
- Formal succession planning program: scope, objectives
- Corporate property
- Executive or human resource reviews: frequency, attendees, process, link to business reviews
- Role of succession planning staff
- Appraisal and development
- High potentials
- Staffing decisions: key decision-makers, nomination strategy, approval authority, CEO role, consideration of individual needs, determination of human resource needs, information sources tapped in candidate assessment, selection criteria
- Cost and effectiveness of succession system

CEO Succession (from former to current CEO)
- Respondent's knowledge of the process
- Decision to replace former CEO
- Key decision-makers
- Timing of the change
- Nominating candidates
- Selection criteria
- Information sources tapped in candidate assessment
- Developing position requirements
- Choosing the successor
- Aftermath of the change

financial statements, important outcomes in this study, are matters of public record. Third, the issue of succession in large corporations is one that compels great interest not only for their members, but for society as a whole. Because of the great power and prestige that attend positions of corporate leadership, choice of these leaders is of substantial consequence for the economic and social well-being of the country. But aside from the glamour and gossip surrounding CEO changes, the burgeoning interest in ensuring executive continuity by firms in this population (noted, for example, by Shaeffer, 1982), and the increasingly large allocation of resources devoted to managing this issue (witnessed in the results of this study), demand that succession systems receive closer scrutiny in this type of organization.

The sample is divided into three types of case: the Target group, the Human Resources Vice Presidents (HRVP) group, and the CEO group. The Target group is so named because reputation data are available for this group only. These are the firms included in the first two years of *Fortune's* annual survey of corporate reputation. To encourage the representatives of this group to respond, they were mailed a letter in advance of the survey indicating that it was to arrive soon. These potential respondents were followed-up on by phone and by mail. And they were invited to a conference at which the results were presented. For every Target group case an HRVP, or equivalent, was identified as a potential respondent. It was assumed that the HRVP would be the most knowledgeable informant about top echelon succession system policies and practices.

The HRVP group includes all non-Targets for which a senior-ranking officer of Human Resources could be identified. The CEO group is the remainder for which the HRVP could not be identified by publicly-available sources, but for which the CEO or President could be. The HRVP and CEO groups received only the survey and cover letter. There was no conference invitation nor was any follow-up done to increase their response rates. The Target group response rate, 56%, was, as expected, much higher than for the non-Targets. Overall response rate was 24.5%. Tests for bias in the sample reveal that respondents and non-respondents do not differ significantly on the financial outcomes and they differ on only one item of the *Fortune* reputation study: community and social responsibility, with respondents scoring higher.

Table II shows the distribution of the sample according to the 25 industries represented. The most frequently represented industries are diversified services, commercial banking, and food. Least frequently represented are mining, apparel, and glass/concrete/abrasives.

On other contextual factors the sample looked like this: (a) average size in revenues or assets = $5.2 billion; (b) average size in number of employees = 37,846; (c) average number of CEOs since the founder (a proxy for age in generations of CEOs) = 4.9; (d) average number of hierarchical levels, from CEO to first line supervisor = 7.1; (e) diversified firms constitute 24 percent of sample; non-diversifieds, 76 percent; (f) firms with a decentralized structure, 63 percent; not decentralized, 37 percent; (g) and the average percentage of inside directors relative to the total number of board members is 31 percent.

Testing for Relationships

In order to test for associations between succession system characteristics and outcomes a series of analyses were conducted. First, the sim-

Table II. Frequency Distribution of Industry for Target and Non-Target Groups.

Industry	Target group	Non-Target group	Total
Aerospace	6	1	7
Apparel	5	0	5
Beverages	6	2	8
Chemicals, Rubber, Plastics, Paint	7	7	14
Commercial Banking	8	12	20
Diversified Financial	6	5	11
Diversified Services	9	14	23
Electronics, Appliances	4	4	8
Food	5	10	15
Forest Products	5	1	6
Glass, Concrete, Abrasives, Gypsum	4	1	5
Industrial, Farm Equipment	7	6	13
Life Insurance	6	2	8
Metal Manufacturing	6	0	6
Metal Products	6	2	8
Mining, Crude-Oil Production	2	2	4
Motor Vehicles and Parts	7	1	8
Office Equipment, Computers	5	1	6
Petroleum Refining	6	3	9
Pharmaceuticals	6	2	8
Precision Instruments	8	1	9
Publishing, Printing	5	1	6
Retailing	6	3	9
Transportation	5	1	6
Utilities	8	5	13
TOTAL	148	87	235

ple correlations between each item in each dimension and all the outcomes were assessed. There are, on average, ten items per dimension, or scale (see Friedman, 1984 for details on scale construction and quality). Then multivariate regressions were performed, using all the items in each scale simultaneously as predictors of each outcome measure. This was done to assess the strengths of the relationships given the effects of other items in the dimension. Finally, those items that retained their relationships with the outcomes in the multivariate tests were included in a second series of multivariate regressions, this time with the contextual factors added. The purpose of doing these analyses was to assess the strengths of relationships over and above the effects of the contextual factors. The succession system correlates of financial performance and corporate reputation reported below are those that were significantly associated in both multivariate tests.

DESCRIPTIVE FINDINGS FOR EACH DIMENSION

In this section, selected findings are presented for each of the seven dimensions that characterize succession systems. The aim of this section is to describe the key elements of succession systems as they exist in the firms in this sample. The hypothesized and observed relationships to the outcomes, those suggested by Arrow 1, are discussed in the following section.

Formalization

Definition: The extent to which prescribed, written rules and procedures exist for the manner in which succession events and the development of leaders are to occur.

Procedures for succession process. Only 27 percent of the firms use some kind of formal procedure for the identification of selection criteria and candidate nomination, the two intermediate stages of the four-stage succession process. An example of such a formal procedure occurs in the General Electric Company (Friedman and LeVino, 1984). The "slate system" at GE calls for the documentation of selection criteria, or job specifications, prior to the search for candidates. When a position opens, a succession planning staff person works with the hiring executive to determine the job specifications. Once this is done, the staff person conducts an internal search for candidates. The centralized inventory of management talent kept at GE is a prime source of information on potential candidates. So are the other succession planning staff who are continually seeking and documenting information about people—their capabilities and developmental needs. A slate of candidates is prepared. It can include people from throughout the company. The hiring executive then interviews and must choose from this slate.

Staff function, replacement plans, executive reviews. About two-thirds of the companies have a staff function specifically responsible for succession planning. Approximately three-quarters maintain replacement plans, or backup lists, for top echelon executives. This same percentage of the 235 companies conduct planned, periodic reviews of management talent at which succession and development issues (e.g., promotability of subordinates) are discussed.

Summary. There appears to be a considerable degree of formalization in the succession systems of the 235 firms in terms of the existence of a succession planning staff, replacement plans, and executive or human resource reviews. However, in the actual process of succession events formal procedures are relatively rare. This distinction is likely due to the longer time period over which formal procedures in succession processes evolve and become an accepted management practice. Indeed, among firms in this sample, 68 percent report having a formal succession plan, but 18 percent have had one for less than two years; they are still maturing. Since such sensitive matters as who shall rule are at stake in succession events, it is likely that to begin to formalize succession processes is to encounter resistance, especially if current norms support nepotism. The time lag, therefore, may account for why formalization is more common in the management practices affecting the process than in the process itself.

Control Systems

Definition: The extent to which a system of checks and balances operates to ensure broad-based representation in, and adequate managerial attention to, succession issues.

Audit of reviews. A key indicator on this dimension is the extent to which there is follow-up and auditing of the executive or human resource review process, if it exists. For instance, if the review is held annually (as it typically is), a semi-annual or quarterly check on the progress of plans might be conducted either by an executive's superior or by a member of the succession planning staff. And at the annual review session one of the key points of discussion might be an audit on the actions taken on developmental plans. Fifty four percent of the companies report that such follow-up occurs to a great extent.

Higher level involvement in succession processes. The involvement of higher levels of management in the four stages of the succession process is another measure of control. Higher level influence is that exerted by the hiring executive's boss and the CEO. The extent to which they are involved as checks on the succession process is greatest in the candidate selection stage (88 percent report a great extent of involvement here). This is intuitively obvious given the importance of the selection stage: it is here that the final decision in a succession event is made. However, having checks and balances on the prior stages is not a trivial matter since the final choice is likely to be determined by the kinds of criteria applied and by the list of candidates. The stage in which higher levels are least involved is candidate nomination: 70 percent of the firms report great involvement by higher levels at this stage.

Evaluation and compensation on subordinate development. Whether or not executives are evaluated on and compensated for their efforts to develop their subordinates is a critical indicator of control. Only 20 percent of the respondents said that executives in their companies are monitored and rewarded, at least in part, on this basis, although about 40 percent said that they are "some of the time." This is an essential means for guaranteeing that executive development gets sufficient attention.

Summary. Executive reviews, though common, are monitored to a great extent only in 54 percent of the companies that conduct them. Such controls, therefore, are not enacted in all firms that have executive reviews. Higher levels of management are usually involved as checks on the quality of succession processes, most frequently in the final stage, selection. Finally, the monitoring and remunerating of executives on the basis of their performance as developers of people, a powerful means by which to ensure adequate attention to succession and development issues, is a relatively uncommon practice.

Resource Allocation

Definition: The extent to which time and energy are devoted to managing succession issues.

Replacement planning. For the firms in this sample, on average, 86 percent of top echelon executives have replacement plans. Sometimes colloquially referred to as "truck lists" (i.e., replacements for the executive if he or she is hit by a truck), these lists of backups are typically for emergency purposes only and do not necessarily represent the optimal slate of candidates in terms of preparedness and availability. In most companies, then, time and energy are devoted to this succession system task.

Frequency of reviews. Another indicator of time spent is the frequency with which executive or human resource reviews are held. Every 10 months is the average; the modal response is "annually." Usually these meetings coincide with other planning cycles (e.g., budget planning and review).

CEO's time spent. The average amount of time spent by the CEO on succession issues as a percentage of his or her total work time is 11 percent. This is an important indicator of resource allocation because it represents energy expended by the most visible, most salient individual in a firm. If the CEO spends time working on matters of development and succession then it is likely that others in the organization do so as well. The CEO can signal to the rest of the organization that these activities deserve attention by serving as a role model.

Placements for development. Perhaps the most subtle indicator of resource allocation is measured in the following question:

Staffing decisions can be based on the needs of the company, the needs of a particular unit, and/or the needs of the individual who is being placed in the position. Of all the staffing decisions made for the top echelon of your company, in what percentage of them does each of these three kinds of needs typically get considered?

Company needs considered   _____ % of the time.
Particular unit needs considered   _____ % of the time.
Individual developmental needs considered   _____ % of the time.

Let us consider the last part only: individual developmental needs. On average they are considered 32 percent of the time. This is a matter of resource allocation because to consider individual developmental needs as a selection criterion is to trade off short-term efficiency in a particular job for long-term developmental benefits for the individual. For example, if two candidates, A and B, are being considered, and A is slightly better qualified to assume the role than B, but B would benefit more from the experience, choosing B would mean a loss in efficiency (B would have more to learn in order to do the job well) but a long-term gain for B in his/her having learned a new set of skills. This, in turn, is to the long-term benefit of the company in the sense that this particular executive will be better prepared to assume roles in the future that demand broad experience. In most cases, then, slots are being filled on the basis of who can do the job best now, rather than on the basis of who will learn the most from the experience. The immediate pressure to have the best person in a job usually outweighs the need to use placements as opportunities to broaden others.

Summary. There is a considerable amount of time and energy devoted to such formal practices as executive reviews and to short-term planning for replacements. CEOs typically spend about 11 percent of their time dealing with succession issues. Investment in the development of future leaders by way of placements-for-growth, however, is not a common practice.

Information Systems

Definition: The extent to which data are gathered from relevant sources on people and positions and are applied in decisions on, or exchanged in reference to, succession and development issues.

Information exchange in reviews. One set of indicators for this dimension has to do with the kinds of information exchanged in executive reviews, if they are held. Promotability of subordinates is the prime topic of discussion. These meetings are forums for the exchange of ideas about the developmental needs of individuals lower in the hierarchy and how to meet them. Also, organization structure is an important topic because reorganizations are often necessary in order to accommodate the shifting of responsibilities among key managers for developmental reasons. In many organizations staffing decisions are actually made in the executive reviews. If, for instance, it is known that a position is soon to be vacated due to an impending retirement, plans for a successor might be explored and confirmed. Information from individuals about their career plans is not as frequently considered as the above issues. This indicates that the typical information exchange about promotability is assymetrical, not balanced, implying a top-down approach to career planning.

Information sources for forecasting needs. The information sources tapped in forecasting future personnel needs is another important aspect of information systems. According to survey respondents, in most instances these forecasts are based on the informal perceptions of key actors; they are not systematic. Yet more than half of the sample companies drew on strategic business plans for this data. This is evidence of attempts to integrate business and human resource planning activities, but the quality of the data exchanged may be low. Environmental scans (e.g., of demographic trends in the external labor market) are not usually conducted for the purpose of forecasting needs, most likely because such research is often done by analysts outside the firm and need not be done internally.

Centralized talent inventories. Centralized inventories of management talent are kept by 77 percent of the 235 firms. These can be valuable sources of information when, for example, creating candidate slates composed of people from diverse parts of a firm. Typically these slates are drawn up by a centralized staff person, as in the case of General Electric. In companies where this occurs there is tension between the centralized staff and the executives responsible for the various business units, especially if the business units are given the mandate to run their own show. The tension arises because ownership of the business by the unit executive is limited when it comes to making critical personnel decisions. The centralized inventory, then, is a valuable tool for exerting corporate control over human resource deployment. (The ownership issue is taken up in more detail in the discussion about the "Staff Role" dimension, below.)

Information flow between periodic human resource and business reviews. In 46 percent of the companies, business reviews precede and provide the basis for discussion in executive reviews. Information from the business reviews about, for example, human resource demands derived from a plan to grow new businesses internally, calls for the analysis of current and future supply to meet these demands. Discussions about promotability of subordinates, for instance, in the human resource reviews are then seen in light of such business plans. Only eight percent of the companies report that the two sets of reviews are independent *and* that they should be. Nearly half, 43 percent, say that the reviews are independent but that they should be more closely linked. In rare cases, three percent, the human resource reviews precede and provide the basis for discussion in the business planning sessions. The philosophy guiding these succession systems might be termed "strategy follows people" (Jack Welch, GE's CEO, quoted in Friedman and LeVino, 1984).

Summary. Human resource reviews tend to focus on the exchange of information about promotability of subordinates, organization structure, and actual placement decisions. Forecasting of human resource supply and demand is based on strategic plans in more than half the companies, but the informal perceptions of key actors are the most common means of gathering such information. Centralized inventories are kept by about three-quarters of the companies. And for the great majority, business reviews either precede and drive discussions in human resource reviews, or, if they do not, then they ought to, according to the respondents.

Political Criteria

Definition: The extent to which selection decisions are based on loyalty, network ties, and other non-ability factors.

The critical distinction between this and the following dimension, "Technical Criteria," is whether or not selection criteria have to do with technical competence given the job requirements. Are selection decisions based on who one knows or what one knows? Cited most frequently as political criteria applied in the typical succession event are coming from within the firm, management style, and willingness to make a total commitment to the firm. Least frequently noted are similarity to the former job incumbent, personal background, and age considerations. According to respondents, then, the nontechnical criteria most frequently applied are not so explicitly political (i.e., based on long-term relationships with key decision-makers) as they are cultural in that they have to do with being part of the ongoing social system, fitting in. The relative importance of political vs. technical criteria likely varies across hierarchical levels; fitting in becomes more critical as one ascends the corporate ladder.

Technical Criteria

Definition: The extent to which selection decisions are based on past performance, range of experience, and other ability factors.

According to survey respondents, the most frequently applied criteria of this type have to do with demonstrated ability to perform well over the course of one's career: outstanding performance over time, knowledge of business and industry, and business acumen. Least often applied are those factors that reflect overly-broad individual work histories; those that include experience and training well beyond that which is critical for the typical executive of a large corporation: experience in the public sector, in other industries, and in the international arena. Perhaps in the future the latter criterion, international experience, will assume greater importance as more and more U.S. firms compete in global markets.

Staff Role

Definition: The extent to which internal and external human resource professionals are involved in the support and management of succession and development issues.

Influence on succession events. In this article, the findings for the Staff Role dimension focus only on the role of internal succession staff. One key issue has to do with the amount of influence brought to bear by succession staff on the four stages of the typical succession event. As one would expect, staff are most influential in the two middle stages, determining selection criteria and nominating candidates. Establishing the need for a position and making the ultimate choice from among candidates are decisions typically influenced to a greater extent by line management.

Credibility and access. The respondents, mostly staff themselves, report that succession staff are seen as credible and have the access needed to perform their jobs well. Surely there is some bias in the responses to these questions, and follow-up studies should gather opinions about these and other issues from multiple respondents in each firm.

Ownership of succession system. Finally, the perceived sense of ownership of succession issues was assessed by asking respondents to rank in order those people in the firm who were seen as having the greatest sense of ownership. Human Resource staff are viewed as being the primary owners in 19 percent of the firms whereas the CEO is ranked first in 62 percent of them. Human Resource staff are ranked first slightly more often than senior line management (i.e., top echelon executives other than the CEO); 18 percent ranked senior line management as having the greatest sense of ownership. Management of succession ought to be a line responsibility. But if this is not consistent with an organization's norms and values, then forcing line ownership is difficult and time-consuming. In firms where line ownership is relatively low, it is likely to increase over time if the CEO demonstrates the importance of paying attention to succession issues and if the reward system is so designed as to encourage it.

Summary. In firms that have internal succession staff the people in these roles do exert influence on succession events, but primarily on the two intermediate stages of succession processes: determining selection criteria and nominating candidates. These staff appear to have the access to needed information and the credibility with line management necessary to function effectively. Finally, ownership of succession system tasks and responsibilities by the CEO is most common; however, Human Resource staff are viewed as responsible for succession issues as frequently as senior line management other than the CEO.

Table III.   Correlates of Reputation and Financial Performance

Formalization
  No relationship with reputation or performance

Control Systems
  + CEO influence on candidate nomination
  + Evaluation and compensation based on subordinate development
  + Higher level influence in succession events
  + Audit of reviews

Resource Allocation
  + CEO's time spent on succession
  + % formally appraised
  + % of time individual needs considered in moves
  + Frequency of reviews

Information Systems
  + Earnestness of reviews
  + Use of environmental scans to forecast needs
  + HR–business reviews linkage

Political Criteria
  No relationship for "network ties" items
  + Inside the company
  + Loyalty
  + Personal values matching company values

Technical Criteria
  + Performance in a particular task
  + Business acumen
  + Negotiation skills

Staff Role
  + Credibility
  + Access
  − Ownership of succession issues
  − Influence on succession events

CORRELATES OF REPUTATION AND FINANCIAL PERFORMANCE

Now that we have reviewed the key descriptive findings, the second research objective can be addressed: Does it matter what a firm's succession system is like? To answer this question, we assess the relationship between the elements of each dimension and two sets of outcomes, reputation and financial performance. Table III lists, for each dimension, those items that are significantly related, either positively or negatively, to these outcomes over and above the effects of contextual conditions. Although they are significant, the strength of the associations listed are, in general, not very great (see Friedman, 1984 for a detailed explanation of the findings for tests of significance). That some relationships are observed, however, does support the basic notion that high vs. low performing firms are different with respect to important aspects of their succession systems.

It was hypothesized that high levels of *Formalization* would be associated with good performance. However, the results do not confirm this. No relationships were observed between Formalization scale items and the outcomes. The mere existence of such formal procedures as annual appraisals, human resource reviews, and replacement plans does not seem to differentiate good and poor performers. We may assert that these procedures are vehicles for the enactment of sound succession practice, but they are not useful unless reinforced by adequate controls, information, resource allocation, appropriate selection criteria, and credible staff. In other words, formalization may be seen as a necessary but not sufficient condition for effective succession systems.

The findings for *Control Systems* are consistent with the hypothesis for this dimension. Statistically significant, positive associations with the outcomes were found for the CEO's influence on candidate nomination, the evaluation and compensation of executives based on how well they develop subordinates, the existence of higher level checks and balances on succession events, and the existence of human resource review audits. There does appear to be a payoff for having controls on the succession system. Without timely reinforcement, succession issues are too easily relegated to the back burner. And in firms where they are not a priority, performance tends to be low.

Resource Allocation dimension results are consistent with the proposed relationships as well. The time spent by the CEO on succession issues and the percentage of employees who actually receive formal appraisals periodically are two indicators of time and energy devoted to succession matters that are positively related to the outcomes. The use of job placements as opportunities to develop people, as indicated by the percentage of time individual needs are considered in staffing moves, is another correlate of high performance. Finally, the frequency with which human resource reviews are held, again, not just their mere existence, discriminates between high and low performing firms. Firms that devote resources to succession issues seem to fare better than those that do not.

The findings for *Information Systems* are consistent with the hypothesized relationship too. The earnestness with which human resource reviews are held, that is, the extent to which they are not just "paper exercises" but do include the exchange of useful, pertinent information about people and positions, is one correlate of good performance. Also, the use of environmental scans to forecast future human resource needs, an indicator of the degree to which human resource planning is systematic, and not haphazard, is significantly associated with high levels of reputation and financial performance. Finally, the linkage between human resource and business reviews, a crucial means by which relevant information about succession issues is exchanged, is another correlate of high performance.

The results for *Political Criteria* are contrary to what was expected. There is no relationship between the items from this dimension representing network ties (i.e., long term relationships with key decision-makers and similarity to the former job incumbent) and the performance outcomes. A negative association was expected on grounds that political placements would result in people-position mismatches, hence poor individual and organizational performance. However, three of the political criteria (i.e., coming from inside the company, demonstrated loyalty, and personal values matching company values) are positively and significantly associated with high performance. These factors seem to indicate the importance of hiring from within. They can be construed as technical criteria of a sort, for having been with a firm for a long time, one knows how to get things done in it. One knows where to get information and resources in order to accomplish objectives. And the ability to hire from within is predicated on the assumption that a sufficient pool of talent exists within an organization from which candidates can be drawn. This occurs when succession and development issues have been given adequate attention in the past.

The findings for *Technical Criteria,* those that are clearly related to a candidate's skills and abilities and not to his/her political and cultural bonds, do support the hypothesis for this dimension, but the observed relationships with outcomes are not as strong as those in the Political Criteria dimension. Here there are three criteria significantly and positively related to performance: a candidate's performance in a particular task, business acumen, and negotiation skills.

Finally, the hypothesis for the *Staff Role* dimension is that a great deal of staff credibility *and* a lack of staff ownership of succession issues ought to be associated with superior performance. The reasoning is that succession staff have a crucial role to play in doing the background work and in facilitating information exchange among key decision-makers, but if the succession system is "just another personnel process"—if there is not line ownership—then those ultimately responsible for succession decisions are not the ones committed to making them. The results support this notion. The credibility of internal succession staff and their access to needed information are both correlates of high performance. And to the extent that staff have a great degree of ownership of, and influence on, succession events, performance tends to be lower.

IMPLICATIONS FOR MANAGING SUCCESSION SYSTEMS

Given the caveat that what has been observed are correlations and not definitive, causal relationships, let us consider the implications of these results for the management of successions systems. High and low performing firms do appear to have different kinds of succession systems.

The following six implications, generalizations with some ground in empirical reality, are drawn from the distinctions discussed above.

The CEO Must Be Involved

One of the more striking sets of findings is the degree to which CEO involvement correlates with outcomes. This is witnessed in the percentage of CEO's time spent on succession issues and in the CEO's influence on various stages of succession events. Although it is nearly a truism to say that top management commitment is a prerequisite for the success of any program of activity, it seems that in the matter of succession systems, it is indeed true.

What can be done to encourage this kind of commitment? One way is to generate a felt need that succession systems must be attended to by raising questions about the consequences of failure to do so. For example, one might ask, "How many placements will be made well in the next five years?" If the answer is "Not too many, we're filling slots with warm bodies" then one might ask, "What costs are associated with this?" A related question: "What costs have been associated with past failures to effectively match people and positions, both in terms of short- and long-term objectives, or with the need to hire from outside the firm?" These questions force one to consider that which visionary leaders regularly do: the future of the firm and the people needed to make it go.

Human Resource Reviews: A Crucial Process

Human resource reviews provide a forum for the exchange of information and ideas about people and (current and future) positions and about how to affect their appropriate match. Too, holding reviews reinforces the idea that executives are accountable for the growth and development of their subordinates. If done well human resource reviews can accomplish a great deal. Developmental needs can be discussed and plans made for meeting them; placement decisions can be analyzed; and the link between strategy, structure, and staffing can be forged. The earnestness with which they are conducted, the frequency of reviews, and the follow-up and audit of them are all important correlates of outcomes in this study. After presiding over a recent series of reviews, GE's Chairman Jack Welch is quoted as having said: "That set of reviews is where it's at! Imagine what we could gain if we doubled the time spent on them." (Friedman and LeVino, 1984). Human resource reviews are a crucial element in managing succession systems.

Substance, Not Form

The mere existence of a formal succession planning program, and of formal procedures for the enactment of succession events appear to be, in themselves, of little value in the effective management of succession systems. Some degree of formalization may be required, but what seems to matter most is a genuine commitment to the body and soul of the issues for which the formal procedures provide the skeleton.

How can substance be obtained? Perhaps most important is accountability. If executives know that their compensation and their ability to ascend the corporate hierarchy depend on their performance as part of the succession system then they are likely to take this aspect of their roles seriously. To illustrate, consider the story of the CEO who, upon assuming his position in a major computer and communications firm, asked his top 35 executives to submit memoranda detailing their efforts to develop their key subordinates over the past year. When this request went out, early in the year, it was ignored by all but one of the new CEO's subordinates. Later that year, when it came time for the CEO to decide on the incentive compensation for each of his subordinates, he told each one that 10 percent of their bonus was to be based on their response to his initial request for data about subordinate development, and that they, except for the one who did respond, were losing that 10 percent this year. Early in the next year, at the time this CEO was about to send out the same request, his desk was flooded with memoranda sent by his 35 key executives outlining what they had been and were doing to ensure that the developmental needs of their subordinates were being met.

This story is but one example of how substance in a succession system can be obtained. Line ownership is the objective. This occurs when there is accountability and when the system produces meaningful results. When critical job placements are made as a part of the system's activities, as an outcome of executive reviews, for example, then the system attains credibility. A senior executive at Citibank has said: "One good placement is worth a thousand memos" in getting people to believe in the succession system. When information collected on people and positions *is used* to inform placement decisions, the system becomes accepted as part and parcel of management practice.

Behind the Scenes: Succession Staff

The role of internal staff in the management of succession systems is a difficult one. Staff must at once be aware of both the needs, abilities, and aspirations of people and the sometimes conflicting demands imposed by the organizations in which they work. Staff must be influential in the system of activities that determines the use of a firm's human assets, but not to the point where they are primarily responsible for it. They must do the background work, facilitating, coordinating, but not leading.

There is the potential for staff to abuse the power that comes with access to information about succession decisions. But responsibility must remain with line management. The moment power is abused it is lost because with the abuse of power comes loss of credibility, and without credibility, staff loses its access to information from the line. Still, staff members must act as advocates at times, being able to form and to provide independent judgements. If staff provide appropriate data then their positions are secure because this data is useful and necessary for the succession system to function well.

Executive Development: The Backbone of Succession Systems

A well-developed cadre of management talent is essential for an effective succession system because it is the pool from which candidates are drawn to fill leadership positions. Evidence in this study points to the importance of being able to hire from within. Insider status and loyalty as selection criteria are strong correlates of superior corporate performance.

In general, when the best person for the job is only to be found outside, it is a sign that the system for executive development has gone awry. Evaluating and compensating managers on their ability to develop subordinates, and using placements as opportunities for people to expand their knowledge are correlates of high performance. Some firms are now experimenting with the practice of explicitly indicating not only what is required in a position when it opens but what the position offers as a developmental experience as well. The succession event then becomes more than just filling a slot with someone who can do the job, but an opportunity for someone to learn from his/her experience in it.

This kind of practice can only emerge in those firms where the philosophy of management development is future-oriented. There must be tolerance for failure if people are to learn. This means potential loss of efficiency in the short run, but long term gain in the breadth and depth of the management talent pool. For the next generation of leaders to be well prepared for their roles, their education must not be given short shrift.

Human Resource Strategy and Business Strategy Are Pieces of the Same Puzzle

In adapting to the vagaries of organizational environments, decision-makers in organizations must be systematic in the use and exchange of pertinent information about business and about people plans. The forecasting of future human resource needs via environmental scans is positively associated with performance; doing so by way of the informal perceptions of key decision-makers is negatively correlated with performance. The effective flow of information to and from human resource and business reviews, too, is associated with good organizational performance. Smart decisions about strategic business plans are made by people in the right place, at the right time. The aim of human resource strategy is in getting them there.

Stewart D. Friedman received his B.A. in Psychology and Literature from the State University of New York at Binghamton. After working as a clinical psychologist at the Dartmouth Medical School he took his Ph.D. from The University of Michigan in Organizational Psychology. He is currently Assistant Professor of Management at The Wharton School, University of Pennsylvania, where he teaches human resource management and organizational behavior to undergraduate and graduate students, and to executives. He has published and presented papers on succession systems, human resource management, culture in organizations, and the dynamics of work teams.

REFERENCES

Carroll, G. R. Dynamics of publisher succession in newspaper organizations. *Administrative Science Quarterly*, 1984, 29(1), 93–113.

Friedman, S. D. *Succession systems and organizational performance in large corporations.* Unpublished doctoral dissertation, University of Michigan, 1984. Revised version published as monograph: *Leadership succession systems and corporate performance.* Center for Career Research and Human Resource Management, Columbia University, 1985.

Friedman, S. D., and Levino, T. P. Strategic appraisal and development at General Electric Company. In C. J. Fombrun, N. M. Tichy, and M. A. Devanna (Eds.), *Strategic Human Resource Management.* New York: Wiley, 1984, 183–202.

Fulmer, R. M. *Presidential succession.* New York: American Management Association, 1978.

Gupta, A. K. Contingency linkages between strategy and general manager characteristics: A conceptual evaluation. *Academy of Management Review*, 1984, 9(3), 339–412.

Hambrick, D. C., and Finkelstein, S. Managerial discretion: A bridge between polar views of organizational outcomes. To appear in B. Staw and L. L. Cummings (Eds.), *Research in Organizational Behavior, Vol. 9.* Greenwich, CT: JAI Press, forthcoming, 1987.

House, R. J., Singh, J. V., and Tucker, D. J. *Some of the causes and effects of executive succession: An ecological perspective.* Paper presented at the 7th EGOS Colloquium, Stockholm School of Economics, Sweden, June 1985.

Lieberson, S., and O'Connor, J. F. Leadership and organizational performance: A study of large corporations. *American Sociological Review,* 1972, 37, 117–130.

Louis, M. R. Organizations as culture-bearing milieux. In L. R. Pondy, P. J. Frost, G. Morgan, and T. C. Dandrige (Eds.), *Organizational symbolism.* Greenwich, CT: JAI Press, 1983, 39–54.

Lundberg, C. The dynamic organizational contexts of executive succession: Considerations and challenges. *Human Resource Management,* 1986, 25(2), this issue.

Makin, C. Ranking corporate reputations. *Fortune*, January 10, 1983.

Perry, W. J. America's most admired corporations. *Fortune*, January 9, 1984.

Pfeffer, J., and Davis-Blake, A. Administrative succession and organizational performance: How administrator experience mediates the succession effect. *Academy of Management Journal*, 1986, 29(1), 72–83.

Pfeffer, J., and Salancik, G. R. *The external control of organizations.* New York: Harper and Row, 1978.

Shaeffer, R. G. *Top management staffing challenges: CEO's describe their needs.* New York: Conference Board, 1982.

Smith, J. E., Carson, K. P., and Alexander, R. A. Leadership: It can make a difference. *Academy of Management Journal*, 1984, 27, 765–776.

Tushman, M. L., Virany, B., and Romanelli, E. *Effects of CEO and executive team succession: A longitudinal analysis.* Unpublished manuscript, Columbia University, November 1985.

Weiner, N. *Organization performance as a function of leadership and situation factors.* Doctoral dissertation, University of Minnesota, 1977. (University Microfilms No. 78-9763).

Zald, M. N. Political economy: A framework for comparative analysis. In M. N. Zald (Ed.), *Power in organizations.* Nashville, TN: Vanderbilt University Press, 1970, 221–261.

Matching Managers to Strategies: Point and Counterpoint*

—— Anil K. Gupta ——

In recent years, an emerging and increasingly popular theme in the strategic management literature has been that the selection of general managers should be tied directly to the strategies of business units they will oversee. Because different strategies imply different priorities and the need for different skills, such a proposition has obvious intuitive appeal. Beyond intuitive appeal and supporting conceptual arguments, recent empirical research on whether matching general managers to strategies "pays off" in terms of more effective strategy implementation has also yielded positive results. Despite this evidence, several arguments exist for why it may not always be feasible, necessary, or desirable to match general managers to strategies. Thus, there is need for a point–counterpoint "debate" on the subject of matching general managers to strategies. Based on a review of the relevant literature, logical reasoning, as well as some case evidence, this paper is intended to be such a debate undertaken by the author with himself. It is hoped that such a dialectical analysis will open up new avenues for productive research and also enable corporate executives to make better "managerial selection" decisions.

> When we classified . . . [our] . . . businesses, and when we realized that they were going to have quite different missions, we also realized that we had to have quite different people running them. That was where we began to see the need to meld our human resource planning and management with the strategic planning we were doing.
>
> Reginald H. Jones, former CEO, General Electric Company (Fombrun, 1982, p. 46).

Echoing Mr. Jones' perspective, the last five years have seen the emergence of a dominant paradigm which argues that, for strategy implementation to be successful, the choice of SBU general managers (or corporate CEOs) should be contingent upon the type of strategy being implemented (e.g., Gupta, 1984; Gupta and Govindarajan, 1984a; Leontiades, 1982; Szilagyi and Schweiger, 1984). The underlying premises behind this viewpoint have been: (1) for effective execution, different

* The support of the Human Resources Policy Institute, School of Management, Boston University, is gratefully acknowledged. Stewart Friedman and N. Venkatraman provided helpful comments on earlier drafts of this paper.

strategies require different skills, knowledge, and values; (2) because they are human, individual general managers are limited in the skills, knowledge, and values they bring to their tasks; thus, (3) the notion of generalist general managers is essentially bankrupt and an *astrategic* assignment of general managers to SBUs or corporations is bound to be suboptimal.

While it would be difficult to argue against these premises, it is striking that, despite arguments and evidence to the contrary, literature on this subject has not even touched upon the possibility that, in many situations, it may be infeasible, pointless, or perhaps dysfunctional to match managers to strategies. History suggests that the bane of many a brilliant idea has been an unduly excessive preference for simplistic rather than complex frameworks—a recent example being Boston Consulting Group's portfolio planning model for determining different strategic missions for different business units (Henderson, 1970; Kiechel, 1982). If the strategy–manager idea is not to meet a similar fate, it is important that arguments *against* matching managers to strategies be put forward just as explicitly as arguments *for* matching.

The objective of this paper is to pursue the much needed dialectical inquiry by reviewing the research literature and extending/positing logical arguments in favor of both opposing positions. Going beyond the debate, the paper also attempts to synthesize the two perspectives so that managers might be left clearer rather than more confused about what to do with respect to matching managers to strategies, and researchers might find new and worthwhile avenues for further inquiry.

ARGUMENTS FOR MATCHING MANAGERS TO STRATEGIES

The primary arguments for matching managers to strategies are: (1) strategies differ across organizations and over time and the relative usefulness of different managerial skills varies across strategic contexts; (2) managers differ in the educational, experience, and personality make-ups—and, thus, skills and orientations—they bring to their positions; and, (3) matching managers to strategies leads to improved performance. The following sections pursue each of these arguments in greater detail.

Strategies Differ

More than 80% of the 500 largest industrial firms in the United States are diversified into more than one business and consequently undertake strategy formulation at at least two levels: corporate and SBU (Rumelt, 1974). Thus, differences in strategic contexts are usefully examined at both the corporate and the SBU levels.

Corporate-Level Strategy: At the corporate level, one of the most significant dimensions along which strategic contexts differ is the extent and type of diversification undertaken by different firms. Following Rumelt (1974), extent of diversification refers to the multiplicity of businesses in which the firm operates and type of diversification refers to the nature of linkages—vertical, horizontal, or none—between these businesses. Thus, Apple Computer, operating only in the personal computer market, exemplifies a nondiversified *single business* firm. International Paper, with businesses ranging from forestry to finished paper, is a good example of a *vertically integrated* firm. AT&T, operating in the computer and telecommunications markets, typifies a *related diversified* firm. Finally, Textron, operating in businesses as varied as helicopters, chain saws, and writing instruments, epitomizes the *unrelated diversified* conglomerate.

Berg (1969), Gupta (1984), Leontiades (1982), Scott (1973), and others have argued that different points along the spectrum from single business to unrelated diversified firms require different priorities, perspectives, and behavior on the part of the CEO. At the single business end, the number of profit centers is limited—often just one—and the boundaries of the external environment are relatively well defined. Thus, the locus of responsibility and initiative regarding decisions about how to compete within the particular industry and what functional strategies (in R&D, manufacturing, marketing, etc.) to pursue rests appropriately with the firm's CEO. In contrast, at the unrelated diversified end, given the large number of businesses, the CEO's primary task becomes portfolio management, i.e., the addition or deletion of businesses and the addition to or reduction in financial resources allocated to the different businesses. As has been correctly posited by Vancil and Lorange (1975), in such a firm the locus of responsibility for decisions regarding how to compete and what functional strategies to pursue within particular markets can and should rest primarily with the various middle-level (SBU) general managers and not with the corporate CEO. Following these arguments, at the single business end, some of the more critical skills for the CEO are extended familiarity with the particular firm and industry, expertise in R&D, manufacturing, or marketing, as well as high interpersonal orientation; in contrast, at the unrelated diversified end, it is skills relating to financial management and *im*personal financial control that become more useful. These and other hypotheses relating to the implications of variations in corporate-level strategy have been discussed in detail in Gupta (1984).

SBU-Level Strategy: Unlike corporate-level strategy, existing conceptualizations of SBU-level strategy are more complex and there is a lesser degree of consensus regarding how best to differentiate one strategic context from another. Nonetheless, there exist conceptualizations of SBU-level strategy that are both widely used in practice and also have received support from theoretical as well as empirical research. Two such conceptualizations are: (1) the SBU's "strategic mission" in the corporate portfolio (Abell and Hammond, 1979; Larreche and Srinivasan, 1982; Hambrick et al., 1982) and (2) the SBU's "competitive strategy" vis-a-vis other firms in the industry (Hambrick, 1983; Porter, 1980).

On the dimension of strategic mission, the two most prominent strategic archetypes are: "build" and "harvest" (Buzzell and Wiersema, 1981; Gupta and Govindarajan, 1984a). A *build* mission, exemplified by Phillip Morris in soft drinks, signifies an intent to increase market share and competitive position even though short-term earnings might be low or negative. In contrast, a *harvest* mission, exemplified by American Brands in its tobacco products business, signifies an intent to maximize short-term earnings and cash flow even though market share may decline. Variations in the relative usefulness of different managerial skills emanate from the market share vs. profitability and cash flow orientations of build vs. harvest SBUs. For build SBUs, given their market share orientation and longer time horizon, skills relating to product–market innovation, entrepreneurial behavior, risk-taking, and human resource development are argued to be more useful; in contrast, for harvest SBUs, whose time horizon for profit maximization is much shorter, it is skills in production and accounting/finance as well as a preference for avoiding innovation and risk that become more useful (Gupta and Govindarajan, 1984a).

On the dimension of competitive strategy, Porter (1985) has identified the two most prominent archetypes as: "differentiation" and "low cost." A strategy of *differentiation*, exemplified by Mercedes in automobiles, indicates a preference for superior product or service attributes as opposed to lower cost. In contrast, a strategy of *low cost*, exemplified by Chevrolet in automobiles and Timex in wrist watches, signifies just the opposite kinds of preferences. Again, variations in the relative usefulness of different managerial skills emanate from the differing priorities of differentiation and low cost strategies. According to Porter (1980), for an SBU pursuing a differentiation strategy, the priority is on "creating something that is perceived *industrywide* as being unique. . . . (Such a) strategy does not allow the firm to ignore costs, but rather they are not the primary strategic target" (p. 37). In contrast, cost leadership "requires aggressive construction of efficient-scale facilities, vigorous pursuit of cost reductions from experience, tight cost and overhead control, avoidance of marginal customer accounts, and cost minimization in areas like R&D, service, sales force, advertising, and so on. A great deal of managerial attention to cost control is necessary to achieve these aims" (Porter, 1980, p. 35). Thus, for a differentiation strategy, industry knowledge, marketing and product R&D skills, and the ability to foster creativity are argued to be more critical; in contrast, it is the ability to maximize internal throughput efficiency through tight operational and financial controls that becomes more critical for the implementation of a low cost strategy (Gupta, 1984).

Managers Differ

The argument that different skills are needed to implement different types of strategies would not be of much salience if general managers came from similar backgrounds and the repertoire of skills and orientations possessed by most general managers was broad enough to enable selective application of different skills in different contexts. However, empirical research is already beginning to demonstrate (1) that general managers differ among themselves in the education, experience, and personality make-ups they bring to their positions and (2) that these differences in background create significant differences in their predispositions toward various strategic activities.

Kotter's (1982) was among the first field studies that began systematically to explode the myth of the universalistic general manager. Titled in the plural—*The General Managers*—this study concluded: "Almost all of the GMs in this study were highly *specialized*. That is, they had personal characteristics that closely fit the specific demands of the contexts in which they worked" (1982, p. 34). Over the years, evidence in support of differences among general managers along both demographic and personality dimensions has continued to mount. Thus, building on Hambrick and Mason's (1984) conceptual work, Grimm and Smith (1985) have reported recently that, in the railroad industry, the age, education, and length of industry experience of top managers varies across firms and that firms with younger, less experienced, but more educated managers tend to pursue relatively more innovative strategies. Similarly, Gupta's (1985) study of the backgrounds of top managers of the 75 largest U.S.-based industrial companies has found that top managers, including CEOs, come from a wide diversity of educational backgrounds and that there is a strong positive association between incidence of MBA education and 5-year appreciation in the company's stock price. Focusing on personality rather than demographic characteristics, Miller et al. (1982) found a similar diversity in chief executives' "locus of control" (i.e., the extent to which executives view themselves, rather than the external environment, as being in control of most situations; see Rotter, 1966). Miller et al. also reported that CEOs with a more internal locus of control tended to pursue more innovative and more risky strategies for their firms. Personality differences among general managers have also been discovered by scholars of similarities and differences between entrepreneurs and nonentrepreneurs. Thus, Brockhaus (1980) has reported that entrepreneurs tend to have higher risk propensities than nonentrepreneurs. Similarly, Schere (1982) has reported that entrepreneurs exhibit a greater tolerance for ambiguity than nonentrepreneurs.

Consistent with these empirical findings, scholars of corporate leadership have also continued to emphasize both that corporate heads (or SBU general managers) are not all alike and that the choice of which individuals come to hold these positions makes a crucial difference to organizational decisions and actions. This emphasis is evident strongly in the hypothesized differences between "leaders" and "managers" (Levinson and Rosenthal, 1984; Zaleznik, 1977) and the recent calls for "transformational leadership" in American industry (Bennis and Nanus, 1985; Burns, 1978). As Tichy and Ulrich (1984) have argued rather eloquently:

> To revitalize organizations such as General Motors, American Telephone and Telegraph, ... just to mention a few companies currently undergoing major transformations—a new brand of leadership is necessary. *Instead of managers* who continue to move organizations along historical tracks, *the new leaders must transform* the organizations and head them down new tracks. What is required of this kind of leader is an ability to help the organization develop a vision of what it can be, to mobilize the organization to accept and work toward achieving the new vision, and to institutionalize the changes that must last over time. Unless the creation of this breed of leaders becomes a national agenda, we are not very optimistic about the revitalization of the U.S. economy (1984, p. 59, emphasis added).

At a more concrete level, accounts in the business press also continue to reinforce the notion that managers do differ and that different managers tend to pursue different strategies. The recent battle between founder Steven Jobs and "professional manager" John Sculley for the control of Apple Computer and its future strategic direction—and the directors' support for Sculley—is just one out of countless such examples (Uttal, 1985).

Matching Managers to Strategies Yields Superior Performance

If different skills and orientations are needed for the effective implementation of different strategies and if different managers generally possess different skills and orientations, it follows that a systematic matching of managers to strategies will yield superior performance. Although empirical research on the *performance* implications of matching managers to strategies has tended to be very sparse, the only evidence that does exist (Gupta and Govindarajan, 1984a) has provided strong support to this general hypothesis. Beyond this empirical and its underlying conceptual support (Gupta, 1984; Leontiades, 1982; Stybel, 1982; Szilagyi and Schweiger, 1984), this proposition also has come to be advocated increasingly by consulting firms (SPI, 1981; Gerstein and Reisman, 1983) and to guide managerial practice. For instance:

> IBM named Philip D. Estridge, 47-year old president
> of its Entry Systems personal computer division in Boca
> Raton, Florida, to a corporate post overseeing world-
> wide manufacturing. *It also appointed William C.
> Lowe, 44 years old, who oversaw IBM's office network strategy, to suc-
> ceed Mr. Estridge as president of Entry Systems. . . .* The
> move indicates a new phase for the personal computer
> business. Mr. Estridge started production, marketing,
> and product development operations. *Mr. Lowe's job will
> be to meld the successful IBM PC family into the rest of IBM's
> extensive computer line. . . .* (Kneale, 1985, p. 14, empha-
> sis added).

The business press has also named Chase Manhattan Bank, Heublein, Texas Instruments, Corning Glass, and General Electric as some of the other companies engaged in linking executive selection with strategic requirements (*Business Week*, 1980). Undoubtedly, the practice is much more widespread than what this small list would suggest. In fact, it might be accurate to conclude that the notion of matching managers to strategies is now rapidly becoming—if it has not already become—an "obvious truism."

ARGUMENTS AGAINST MATCHING MANAGERS TO STRATEGIES

Perhaps because the idea of matching managers to strategies is so intuitively appealing, the question of whether, in some situations, it may be infeasible, pointless, or even dysfunctional to match managers to strategies has remained completely unexplored. This paper argues that at least four factors constrain the utility of matching managers to strategies. These are: (1) need for strategic flexibility, (2) need for management development, (3) motivational problems, and (4) lack of managerial discretion.

Need for Strategic Flexibility

It is obvious that selecting a general manager to fit a particular strategy would be justified only if the strategy selected is an appropriate one. From the perspective of this paper, instances where inappropriate strategies result from poor strategic analysis of the firm and/or its external environment are not of particular significance; in such cases, the prescription would be to redo the strategic analysis and then to match managerial selection to the more appropriate strategy. The more intractable problem arises when high uncertainties regarding environmental opportunities and threats prevent the development of high confidence in *any* strategy. Such situations demand flexibility and an attempt to match general managers to the current strategy is likely to prove unduly constraining.

Low confidence in strategies can be the result of several factors: (1) The environment is constantly evolving and, because of their greater complexity, some markets (such as factory automation) may be inherently more unpredictable than others (such as frozen foods). The more unpredictable a market environment, the more uncertain the viability of a strategy is likely to be. (2) Strategies are formulated not on the basis of what the objective environment really is but on the basis of what it is perceived to be. Because of everpresent managerial biases, these perceptions might often be severely distorted, further reducing corporate executives' confidence in currently formulated strategies. Finally, (3) since environmental conditions serve not only as inputs to strategy formulation but, in reverse, also are influenced by the chosen strategies, all strategies have some probability of becoming self-fulfilling prophecies. In situations where firm-specific factors such as sheer size or political connections or an innovative technology can significantly alter the very environments to which the organization must then respond, the selected strategies have a high probability of being either "very right" or "very wrong."

As a concrete illustration of the need for strategic flexibility, consider the "decline" stage of the product life cycle (Levitt, 1965). If we take the notion of product life cycles to be valid, then we do know that "introduction" leads to "growth" which leads to "maturity" and which is ultimately followed by "decline." However, do we really know what comes after "decline"? As Harrigan (1981) has so convincingly argued and illustrated, the conventional wisdom that "decline" is followed by industry "death" and that all businesses at this stage should be harvested for cash flow is largely a false myth. Depending on one's judgment about how the industry will evolve and the firm's competitive position in it, viable alternative strategies even in apparently declining industries may range all the way from "build" to "niche-based repositioning" to "harvest" to an early "divest." For example:

> Yamaha in the musical instrument market in the U.S. and Honda, Kawasaki, Suzuki, and Yamaha in the motorcycle market in the U.S. and Western Europe have successfully destroyed the dominance of incumbent manufacturers who concentrated on "milking" their products for profit in a stagnant market rather than on fighting a defensive battle to maintain their market share (James, 1984, p. 58).

> Financially oriented U.S. manufacturers once treated the radio as essentially a dot on a product portfolio matrix. Convinced that every product has a life cycle, they viewed the radio as having passed its peak and being a

> prime candidate for "milking." Starved of investment
> funds and resources, the radio died in a self-fulfilling
> prophecy. On the other hand, Japanese radio manufac-
> turers such as Matsushita (Panasonic) and Sony—ignor-
> ing or unaware of product life cycle and portfolio theo-
> ries—obstinately believed in their product's value. The
> division heads of these firms had no option but to ex-
> tend the life of the product since to do otherwise would
> mean dissolving their divisions, which was an unten-
> able option. So they pressed their product engineers,
> component manufacturers, and marketing people for
> new ideas. . . Today the portable radio-cassette and
> Sony "Walkman" stories are part of business folklore
> (Ohmae, 1982, p. 28).

Fascinating as these developments in the musical instruments, motor-
cycle, and radio markets might be, not all industries start out on a
"new" life cycle after a decline in the previous one. More traditional
examples, such as horse-drawn buggies, vacuum tubes, and CB radios
do exist; continued investment in these businesses would almost surely
have proven disastrous for their parent corporations. Thus, it is not
inconceivable that, for many SBUs in declining industries, corporate
executives may choose at least initially to maintain a posture of "strategic flexibility" rather than to commit the firm prematurely either to a
build or to a harvest or to any other specific strategy. Consequently, in
such situations, any attempt to match general managers to specific strategies could well prove dysfunctional.

The need for strategic flexibility might also exist at other stages in the
product life cycle. This would be true particularly in those contexts
where transitions from one stage to another occur rapidly and unpre-
dictably—a recent good example being the personal computer industry
since 1980. Although systematic empirical studies on this subject have
yet to be conducted, commentators such as Fraker (1984), Naisbitt
(1982), and Toffler (1970) seem unanimous in their observation that, in
general, product life cycles are getting shorter. The shorter the product
life cycle and the more unpredictable the transitions from one stage to
another, the more difficult it would be for senior executives or directors
to keep matching managers to the evolving strategies. In such situations, the more viable and attractive option might well be to maximize
strategic flexibility by appointing "generalist" general managers.

Need for Management Development

Management development needs imply that, to prepare an individual
for more senior positions in the corporate hierarchy, it may often be
desirable to deliberately *mis*match—rather than match—managers to
strategies.

Given pyramidal structures, the number of SBUs that an executive oversees must inevitably increase at higher levels in the corporate hierarchy. At General Electric, for instance, in 1981, the head of the Battery Business Department managed just one SBU, the sector executive for the Services and Materials Sector oversaw seven SBUs, while the chief executive of the company was responsible for all of the 38 SBUs (Aguilar and Hamermesh, 1981). Invariably, an increase in the number of SBUs being managed will also imply an increase in the diversity of strategic contexts across these SBUs. In such situations, if the group, sector, or chief executive's prior career experience were to be confined narrowly to just one particular type of strategic context—e.g., creating new businesses or maximizing short-term cash flow—the probability is high that those SBUs whose strategies are "foreign" to the executive's experience will get either neglected or mismanaged through over/under-control. Consequently, in most corporations, exposure to and experience at managing *different* kinds of strategies and businesses needs to be viewed as an essential component of managerial development. As part of this development process, "fast track" middle-level managers would often need to be put also in charge of SBUs to which they are, in an *a priori* sense, *mis*matched. As a secondary benefit, such mismatching also has the potential to yield serendipitously fresh ideas for the strategic positioning of existing SBUs. As John Akers, the chief executive of IBM Corporation, observed recently: "We change because we think we can do a better job. We also change simply to change. It's good to throw the cards up in the air once in a while. The results are often very healthy" (Kindel and Slutsker, 1985).

In addition to increasing the vertical mobility of managers and encouraging a fresh review of existing strategies, horizontal rotation of SBU general managers across *different* strategic contexts may also be a useful administrative mechanism for managing interlinkages among SBUs. As Porter (1985) has argued at length, the synergistic benefits from sharing of skills and resources across SBUs (e.g., a common R&D facility or a common distribution system) can yield significant competitive advantages to the SBUs involved. However, the realization of these synergistic benefits depends critically on how the multi-SBU cluster is coordinated and the speed with which conflicts among the SBUs are resolved (Gupta and Govindarajan, 1986). Based on Galbraith's (1973) arguments, it follows that lateral transfers of managers across SBUs within the cluster would have major benefits in terms of an enhanced appreciation for the needs of different SBUs and hence smoother coordination and conflict resolution. A policy of many lateral transfers would generally work counter to the notion of matching specific managers to specific strategic contexts. It also follows that the idea of matching managers to strategies is likely to have less relevance in the case of SBUs with high interlinkages. Significantly, empirical research has indicated that the incidence of

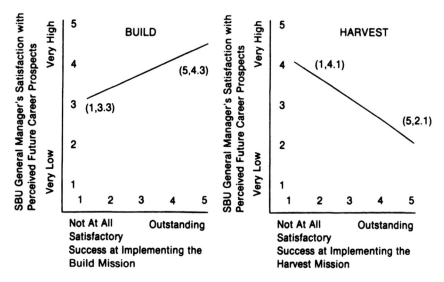

Figure 1. Relationship between success at strategy implementation and satisfaction with perceived future career prospects: Results from a survey of 58 SBU general managers. Source: Adapted from Gupta, A. K. & Govindarajan, V. Build, Hold, Harvest: Converting Strategic Intentions Into Reality. *The Journal of Business Strategy*, 4(3), 1984, 34–47.

interlinkages among SBUs is increasing rather than decreasing (Rumelt, 1974).

Motivational Problems

In light of the fact that some well-regarded corporations—notably General Electric, Corning Glass, Texas Instruments, and Chase Manhattan Bank—have begun to track SBU strategies and managerial skills/orientations systematically in order to assure appropriate matching of the two at *all* times (*Business Week*, 1980), it is important to recognize explicitly the severe motivational problems that such matching can create for many managers—specifically those who get classified as risk-averse "harvesters."

Figure 1, based on actual data from the general managers of 58 SBUs in eight Fortune 500 firms, illustrates the conflict between *corporate* and *individual* returns quite starkly. As expected, those SBU managers who had done a demonstrably effective job at executing a "build" strategy were more satisfied with their future career prospects than those who had not been able to implement a "build" strategy effectively. Notably, however, in the case of "harvest" SBUs, the results were exactly the opposite. In fact, those managers who had done an outstanding job at executing a "harvest" strategy were the ones who reported the greatest degree of *dis*satisfaction with their future career prospects. It would seem that, having done an outstanding job in terms of cash flow and profit maximization, these managers developed expectations of career rewards—expectations that were *systematically* not fulfilled by corporate executives concerned primarily with matching human resource planning to strategic planning. While "harvesting" a subset of all SBUs in the corporation might seem to be rational, it is a rare group of corporate executives who would deliberately decide to "harvest" the entire firm for an extended period of time. Thus, despite the need for a broad-based strategic background at higher levels in the corporate hierarchy, a record of successfully executing a "build" strategy is more likely to increase upward mobility than one of executing a "harvest" strategy. In a telling illustration of this reality, the following speculation regarding who might succeed Walter Wriston as the next CEO of Citicorp appeared in the business press nearly three years *before* the actual announcement of the successor:

> Ironically, Mr. Theobald may not get to the top pre-cisely because he runs a division that has always been a big moneymaker for Citicorp, its institutional division. Unlike his two competitors, who are charting new courses for Citicorp, Mr. Theobald is simply carrying forward a tradition of profiting handsomely from mak-ing loans to corporations and governments, domesti-cally and abroad (Salamon, 1981, p. 1).

Subsequent events have indeed confirmed these speculations. Motivational problems and managerial departures in the Apple II division after then chief executive Steven Jobs' decision to "harvest" this SBU in order to "build" the McIntosh division provide another good example (Wise and Lewis, 1985). It is true that one can also find examples of onetime harvest managers who got promoted to the highest positions in their companies. Nonetheless, the above arguments and data indicate that at least the odds are stacked clearly against the harvest manager.

From a corporate perspective, one approach to dealing with these motivational problems is to accept them for what they are and to miti-gate their dysfunctional effects by appointing older and "clearly pla-teaued" managers to implement harvest strategies and by instituting higher bonuses as a substitute for career rewards. However, in many relatively newer companies—particularly those in the high technology sector—"clearly plateaued" managers may simply not exist; further, the more effective managers may prefer to leave rather than risk becoming (or being viewed as) just good harvesters. In situations such as these, the only viable human resource policy may be to remain flexible about the whole notion of matching general managers to strategies. Gupta and

Govindarajan (1984b) cite the group vice president of an electronic components manufacturer faced with this reality:

> I grant that different kinds of strategies require differ-
> ent kinds of skills. Still, we don't have a very rigid differ-
> entiation of general managers across SBUs. What we do,
> however, is that if we see a weakness in the SBU man-
> ager with respect to his strategy, we try to supplement
> him with an appropriate supporting cast. For instance,
> one of our super-thrust type managers is currently
> heading a sustain business. We have given him a very
> strong controller. This partly helps us transfer general
> managers freely across SBUs so as to round them out
> and probably mitigates some of the motivational prob-
> lems associated with just managing a sustain business
> throughout one's career (p. 41).

Limited Latitude for Action

The root premise behind all of the above arguments—both for *and*
against matching general managers to strategies—has been that the
choice of general managers (or CEOs) makes a *significant* difference to
organizational performance. Despite the "obviousness" of such a premise, it is important to note that research support for it has been decidedly
mixed (Brown, 1982). For example, the empirical studies of Lieberson
and O'Connor (1972) and Salancik and Pfeffer (1977) pointed out that
factors other than choice of organizational leaders (e.g., the economy,
the industry) account for much greater variance in organizational performance relative to the variance explained by leadership alone. Such empirical findings even led Pfeffer (1977) to propose that the selection of
organizational leaders (such as general managers or CEOs) is largely a
symbolic ritual without much substantive import. If so, then the whole
idea of matching general managers to strategies would get reduced to
the status of a non-issue.

In contrast to these symbolic views of leadership, many recent studies
on this subject have tended to conclude that the choice of general managers does have a significant impact on organizational performance. In a
replication of Lieberson and O'Connor's (1972) study—but with an improved methodology—Weiner & Mahoney (1981) reported that corporate stewardship accounted for approximately 44% of the variance in
corporate profitability and 47% of the variance in stock prices! Similarly,
on the basis of a 20-year longitudinal study, Smith et al. (1984) reported
that while organizational performance was not influenced by the mere
event of a change in leadership, it was influenced by the specific choice
of *who* the new leader was. Consistent with these studies' results, Friedman (1984) also reported recently that appropriately designed succession systems are indeed associated with superior performance.

The appropriate conclusion to draw from these conflicting sets of studies would seem to be neither that general managers are impotent nor that they are omnipotent. More likely, perhaps, the typical general manager's latitude for action falls somewhere between zero and infinity. As Hambrick and Finkelstein (1987) have proposed, environmental, institutional, and personal factors can have a systematic impact on whether a general manager's latitude for action ends up being high, moderate, or low. The empirical results of Sheridan et al. (1984) also support such a perspective; they found, for example, that the leader's influence was far greater in contexts where organizational members' rewards were tied to performance than in those other contexts where the performance-reward linkage was weak. Thus, from the perspective of this paper, if the subject of matching managers to strategies is not a non-issue in all cases, it is certainly so in at least a part of them.

Specifically, some of the contextual factors that may reduce a general manager's latitude for action are: (1) significant external regulation, e.g., the electric utility industry today or the airline industry before 1978; (2) powerful buyers or suppliers, e.g., an auto parts manufacturer supplying to General Motors; (3) lack of slack resources, e.g., in the case of high operating and/or financial leverage; (4) a strong corporate culture that tends to "predefine" the required managerial behavior; and (5) tight control by the GM's superiors, e.g., by corporate executives over an SBU general manager or by the board of directors over a corporate CEO. In such low discretion contexts, differences in personal attitudes and expectations might have a significant impact on whether the GM feels more or less frustrated with his/her limited latitude for action; however, these individual differences are less likely to influence *organizational* performance either favorably or unfavorably. To conclude, the general importance of matching managers to strategies might be more limited than would at first appear.

MATCHING MANAGERS TO STRATEGIES: A SYNTHESIS

There are several conclusions to be drawn from the dialectical arguments presented so far: (1) Different strategic contexts imply differing task priorities and the need for different skills and orientations. (2) General managers differ in the demographic and personality backgrounds—hence skills and orientations—that they bring to their positions. (3) In highly unpredictable contexts where senior executives' (or directors') confidence in any strategy is likely to be low, an attempt to match managerial selection to the current strategy would unduly constrain strategic flexibility. (4) The need for broad-based strategic experience (essential for upward mobility and for smoother inter-SBU coordination) would often imply the need to mismatch rather than match managers to strategies. (5) A strict matching of managers to strategies is likely to demotivate some managers—particularly those typecast as "good harvesters." And, (6) in those contexts where managerial discretion is low, matching managers to strategies would be largely a non-issue.

The research implications of these conclusions are fairly straightforward. Since this is the first such dialectical analysis on the subject of matching managers to strategies, many of the conclusions—particularly those against the salience of or need for strategy–manager linkages— need to be tested empirically before they can be regarded as more definitively "true." However, since managerial selection decisions must continue to be made before any such empirical research results are in, managers are likely to be in need of interim guidelines. In view of this need, given below are some practical implications that directors, corporate executives, and human resource managers might draw from these conclusions.

Pay Attention to the Situational Context

Perhaps the most important implication of this point–counterpoint debate is that the situational context matters. As summarized pictorially in Figure 2, depending on the context, matching managers to strategies may be any of several things: a non-issue, unduly constraining, counterproductive, or just the right thing to do. In a majority of contexts, matching managers to strategies would indeed be the best course of action. However, if managerial latitude for action is likely to be low, nonstrategic considerations (e.g., reward for previous accomplishments, cultural "fit," or even seniority) might appropriately be viewed as the more important basis for the selection of general managers. In contexts where discretion would be high but *a priori* confidence in any strategy is very low, it may be best to maintain high degrees of freedom by picking "generalist" general managers—if they exist! Finally, in contexts where organizational performance is satisfactory and some short-term inefficiencies in strategy implementation can be tolerated for the sake of managerial development, the recommended course of action might be to deliberately *mis*match managers to strategies; that may well be the only effective way to groom competent senior executives and "generalist" general managers—without having to go outside (Friedman, 1986).

Go After Intended—Not Current—Strategies

When the context does call for matching managers to strategies, it is most critical to remember that the matching should be to the SBU or corporation's "intended" (i.e., future) and not the "de facto realized" (i.e., current) strategy. Lest this guideline appear too obvious, take the case of two corporations—one a single business firm (such as General

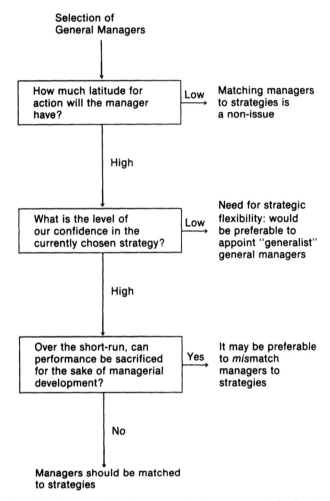

Figure 2. The impact of situational context on managerial selection decisions.

Motors in the early 1980s) and the other an unrelated diversified conglomerate (such as Textron in the early 1980s). The selection of individuals who might best serve as CEOs of these two firms needs to be guided not by how diversified or nondiversified each firm currently is but by the *direction* in which each company's diversification strategy is *intended* to move. If the intended strategy of the single business firm is to become more diversified and that of the conglomerate is to become a more integrated corporation by shedding unrelated businesses, then the single business firm may be headed best by a CEO with a financial background who prefers to manage through *impersonal* controls; in contrast, the conglomerate may be headed best by an operations-oriented "hands-on" manager. In both cases, the recommendations based on intended strategies are totally contrary to what a focus on the current de facto strategies would have incorrectly implied.

As another example, consider the case of an SBU (such as Campbell's soup business) in the maturity stage of the product life cycle. If the CEO of Campbell Soup makes a conscious decision to "build" the soup business despite the apparent maturity of the soup market, the more appropriate manager to head this SBU would seem to be a risk-taker with a marketing background rather than a risk-averse individual with a production or accounting/finance background. A focus on just the "current" stage of the product life cycle would have led to a totally opposite—and incorrect—managerial selection decision.

Focus on the Team—Not Just One Individual

Since considerations other than SBU or corporate strategy (such as nonavailability of "matched" managers, a policy of only internal promotions, the need to develop managers with broad strategic experience, the need for lateral transfers in order to facilitate inter-SBU coordination) will often influence the selection of general managers, a focus on selecting just the one individual "correctly" is bound to be unduly constraining. It is true that the general manager would usually be the single most influential individual in the organization. However, both logical reasoning (Thompson, 1967) and empirical evidence (Hambrick, 1981) indicate that, in most large organizations, absolute power does not reside with the chief executive or SBU head; rather, power is shared by several managers constituting a dominant coalition. Thus, the focus of the key decision makers in any succession event should be at least as much on matching the dominant coalition to the intended strategy as on matching the individual general manager to the intended strategy. When considerations other than business strategy (such as horizontal rotation of general managers in order to foster management development) prevent the selection of a "matched" general manager, the selection of a team of appropriately matched "second lieutenants" might be the most effective course of action.

CONCLUSIONS

Nearly five years ago, the business press observed:

> Manpower planning and strategic planning have become two of the most popular catchphrases in management parlance. . . All too often, however, chief executives speak of manpower and strategic planning as though they were separate functions. Management experts warn that corporations failing to link the two concepts may be sounding the death knell for both (*Business Week*, 1980, p. 166).

It should be a matter of some pride for scholars and executives that, over the intervening period, significant conceptual as well as empirical research has been done to develop both theoretical frameworks and practical guidelines for matching managers to strategies. In fact, it is developments such as these that have led to the emergence of a whole new sub-field called "strategic human resource management." Rooted in these developments, the objective of this paper has been to discourage the adoption of simple-minded approaches towards matching managers to strategies. Specifically, the paper has recommended that, in *some* specific types of situations, instead of matching managers to strategies, it may be wiser to select managers on the basis of nonstrategic considerations, or to select "generalist" general managers, or even to deliberately mismatch managers to strategies.

Anil K. Gupta is Assistant Professor of Organizational Strategy and Policy at the College of Business and Management, University of Maryland at College Park. His research interests include the implementation of multiple business unit strategies within the diversified firm, linkages between organizational strategy and executive leadership, organizational learning, and industry self-regulation. His papers on these topics have been published in several journals including Academcy of Management Journal, Academy of Management Review, *and* Journal of Business Strategy. *He received a D.B.A. from the Graduate School of Business Administration, Harvard University.*

REFERENCES

Abell, D. A., and Hammond, J. S. *Strategic Market Planning.* Englewood Cliffs, NJ: Prentice-Hall, 1979.

Aguilar, F. J., and Hamermesh, R. *General Electric—Business Development.* Boston, MA: Harvard Business School, Case Monograph No. 9-382-092, 1981.

Bennis, W., and Nanus, B. *Leaders.* NY: Harper & Row, 1985.

Berg, N. A. What's Different About Conglomerate Management. *Harvard Business Review,* **45**(6), 1969, 112–120.

Brockhaus, R. H. Sr. Risk-Taking Propensity of Entrepreneurs. *Academy of Management Journal,* **23**, 1980, 509–520.

Brown, M. C. Administrative Succession and Organizational Performance: The Succession Effect. *Administrative Science Quarterly,* **27**, 1982, 1–16.

Burns, J. M. *Leadership.* NY: Harper & Row, 1978.

Business Week, Wanted: A Manager to Fit Each Strategy. February 25, 1980, 166–173.

Buzzell, R. D., and Wiersema, F. D. Modelling Changes in Market Share: A Cross-Sectional Analysis. *Strategic Management Journal,* **2**, 1981, 27–42.

Fombrun, C. Conversation with Reginald H. Jones and Frank Doyle. *Organizational Dynamics,* **10**(3), 1982, 42–63.

Fraker, S. High-Speed Management for the High-Tech Age. *Fortune,* March 5, 1984, 62–68.

Friedman, S. D. *Succession Systems and Organizational Performance in Large Corporations.* Unpublished doctoral dissertation, The University of Michigan, Ann Arbor, 1984.

Friedman, S. D. Succession systems in large corporations: Characteristics and correlates of performance. *Human Resource Management,* **25**(2), 1986.

Galbraith, J. R. *Designing Complex Organizations.* Reading, MA: Addison-Wesley, 1973.

Gerstein, M., and Reisman, H. Strategic Selection: Matching Executives to Business Conditions. *Sloan Management Review,* 24(2), 1983, 33–49.

Grimm, C. M., and Smith, K. G. Management Characteristics, Strategy, and Strategic Change. Paper presented at the 5th annual Strategic Management Society Conference, Barcelona, Spain, October 1985.

Gupta, A. K. Contingency Linkages Between Strategy and General Manager Characteristics: A Conceptual Examination. *Academy of Management Review,* 9, 1984, 399–412.

Gupta, A. K. *Top Management Background: A Study of the Fortune 75.* Special report prepared at the request of Monsanto Company. Boston, MA: School of Management, Boston University, 1985.

Gupta, A. K., and Govindarajan, V. Business Unit Strategy, Managerial Characteristics, and Business Unit Effectiveness at Strategy Implementation. *Academy of Management Journal,* 27, 1984a, 25–41.

Gupta, A. K., and Govindarajan, V. Build, Hold, Harvest: Converting Strategic Intentions Into Reality. *The Journal of Business Strategy,* 4(3), 1984b, 34–47.

Gupta, A. K., and Govindarajan, V. Resource Sharing Among SBUs: Strategic Antecedents and Administrative Implications. *Academy of Management Journal,* 29(4), 1986, forthcoming.

Hambrick, D. C. Environment, Strategy, and Power Within Top Management Teams. *Administrative Science Quarterly,* 26, 1981, 253–275.

Hambrick, D. C. High Profit Strategies in Mature Capital Goods Industries. *Academy of Management Journal,* 26, 1983, 687–707.

Hambrick, D. C., and Finkelstein, S. Managerial Discretion: A Bridge Between Polar Views of Organizational Outcomes. Forthcoming in L. L. Cummings & B. Staw (Eds.). *Research in Organizational Behavior,* Vol. 9. Greenwich, CT: JAI Press, 1987.

Hambrick, D. C., MacMillian, I. C., and Day, D. L. Strategic Attributes and Performance in the BCG Matrix: A PIMS-Based Analysis of Industrial Product Businesses. *Academy of Management Journal,* 25, 1982, 510–531.

Hambrick, D. C., and Mason, P. A. Upper Echelons: The Organization as a Reflection of Its Top Managers. *Academy of Management Review,* 9, 1984, 193–206.

Harrigan, K. R. *Strategies for Declining Industries.* Lexington, MA: Lexington Books, 1981.

Henderson, B. D. *Perspectives on the Product Portfolio.* Boston, MA: Boston Consulting Group, 1970.

James, B. G. Strategic Planning Under Fire. *Sloan Management Review,* Summer 1984, 57–61.

Kiechel, W. III. Corporate Strategies Under Fire. *Fortune,* December 27, 1982, 34–39.

Kindel, S., and Slutsker, G. Think Again. *Forbes,* November 4, 1985, 38–40.

Kneale, D. Estridge Named to Head IBM's Manufacturing. *The Wall Street Journal,* March 13, 1985, p. 14.

Kotter, J. P. *The General Managers.* NY: The Free Press, 1982.

Larreche, J, and Srinivasan, V. Stratport: A Model for the Evaluation and Formulation of Business Portfolio Strategies. *Management Science,* 28, 1982, 979–1001.

Leontiades, M. Choosing the Right Manager to Fit the Strategy. *The Journal of Business Strategy,* 3(2), 1982, 58–69.

Levinson, H., and Rosenthal, S. *CEO: Corporate Leadership in Action.* New York: Basic Books, 1984.

Levitt, T. Exploit the Product Life Cycle. *Harvard Business Review,* 43(6), 1965, 81–94.

Lieberson, S., and O'Connor, J. F. Leadership and Organizational Performance: A Study of Large Corporations. *American Sociological Review,* **37**, 1972, 117–130.

Miller, D., Kets de Vries, M. F., and Toulouse, J. M. Top Executive Locus of Control and Its Relationship to Strategy-Making, Structure, and Environment. *Academy of Management Journal,* **25**, 1982, 237–253.

Naisbitt, J. *Megatrends.* NY: Warner Books, 1982.

Ohmae, K. The Long and Short of Japanese Planning. *The Wall Street Journal,* January 18, 1982, p. 28.

Pfeffer, J. The Ambiguity of Leadership. *Academy of Management Review,* **2**, 1977, 104–112.

Porter, M. E. *Competitive Strategy.* NY: The Free Press, 1980.

Porter, M. E. *Competitive Advantage.* NY: The Free Press, 1985.

Rotter, J. B. General Expectancies for Internal Versus External Control of Reinforcement. *Psychological Monographs,* **80**, 1966, No. 609.

Rumelt, R. P. *Strategy, Structure, and Economic Performance.* Boston, MA: Division of Research, Harvard Business School, 1974.

Salamon, J. Challenges Lie Ahead for Dynamic Citicorp After the Wriston Era. *The Wall Street Journal,* December 18, 1981, p. 1.

Salancik, G. R., and Pfeffer, J. Constraints on Administrative Discretion: The Limited Influence of Mayors on City Budgets. *Urban Affairs Quarterly,* **12**, 1977, 475–498.

Schere, J. L. Tolerance of Ambiguity as a Discriminating Variable Between Entrepreneurs and Managers. *Proceedings of the 42nd Annual Meeting of the Academy of Management,* New York, 1982, 404–408.

Scott, B. R. The Industrial State: Old Myths and New Realities. *Harvard Business Review,* **51**(2), 1973, 133–148.

Sheridan, J. E., Vredenburgh, D. J., and Abelson, M. A. Contextual Model of Leadership Influence in Hospital Units. *Academy of Management Journal,* **27**, 1984, 57–78.

Smith, J. E., Carson, K. P., and Alexander, R. A. Leadership: It Can Make a Difference. *Academy of Management Journal,* **27**, 1984, 765–776.

SPI, *The Right Manager for the Strategic Mission,* Cambridge, MA: Strategic Planning Institute, 1981.

Stybel, L. J. Linking Strategic Planning and Management Manpower Planning. *California Management Review,* **25**(1), 1982, 48–56.

Szilagyi, A. D. Jr., and Schweiger, D. M. Matching Managers to Strategies: A Review and Suggested Framework. *Academy of Management Review,* **9**, 1984, 626–637.

Thompson, J. D. *Organizations in Action.* NY: McGraw-Hill, 1967.

Tichy, N. M., and Ulrich, D. O. The Leadership Challenge: A Call for The Transformational Leader. *Sloan Management Review,* Fall 1984, 59–68.

Toffler, A. *Future Shock.* NY: Bantam Books, 1970.

Uttal, B. Behind the Fall of Steve Jobs. *Fortune,* August 5, 1985, 20–24.

Vancil, R. F., and Lorange, P. Strategic Planning in Diversified Companies. *Harvard Business Review,* **53**(1), 1975, 81–93.

Weiner, N., and Mahoney, T. A. A Model of Corporate Performance as a Function of Environmental, Organizational, and Leadership Influences. *Academy of Management Journal,* **24**, 1981, 453–470.

Wise, D. C., and Lewis, G. C. A Split That's Sapping Morale at Apple. *Business Week,* March 11, 1985, 106–108.

Zaleznik, A. J. Managers and Leaders: Are They Different? *Harvard Business Review,* **55**(3), 1977, 67–80.

Dilemmas in Linking Succession Planning to Individual Executive Learning*

———— Douglas T. Hall ————

This paper examines the issue of linking the selection of top-level executives with the development of these people. It first describes three stages in an organization's development of a succession system which promotes the attainment of a firm's objectives: 1) one-position staffing, 2) replacement planning, and 3) succession planning. Then we examine the other piece to be connected to succession planning: executive learning. It is argued that most planned executive development is aimed at task learning, not personal learning. Consistent with this condition, most executive education activities overstress classroom-style receptive methods, while neglecting active learning. Reasons for this state of affairs are proposed. The paper concludes with recommendations for enhancing personal learning for executives and for better integrating this learning with the strategic succession planning of the organization. This sort of strategic approach to executive succession is seen as the "acid test" in a firm's strategic planning process.

This article will examine a rare phenomenon: connecting the selection of top-echelon executives with the education and development of those key organizational resources. With strong current interest in improving the succession process in many organizations, there has been a growing awareness of the need to find better methods to identify future leaders, but we must find better ways to develop and to nurture them to candidate status as well. We also need to expand the concept of executive development to encompass *personal learning* as well as task learning. It is argued that the more a succession system promotes all facets of an executive's career growth, the more successful that system will be. This paper will explore some of the dilemmas involved in the succession-development connection.

* This paper was supported in part by the Human Resources Policy Institute at Boston University. The author would like to acknowledge the helpful comments of Chris Argyris, Wendy Cohen, Stewart Friedman, and Kathy Kram on early drafts of the paper. This paper is related to an ongoing study of succession systems conducted with Fred K. Foulkes.

THE SUCCESSION PROBLEM(S)

The One-Position Staffing Stage

The nature of the succession problem depends upon what stage in the evolution of its succession system the organization is in. If the organization is in the early stages of developing formal succession methods, the problem may be that there is no succession planning process at all. Key decision-makers are in a reactive mode: as critical positions become open through departures, retirements, disability, etc., the method used is the *one-position staffing approach: how can we find the best qualified individual for this particular job?* There is little concern for developing the candidate, because there is no time to do so. He or she must be ready now to meet the demands of this higher-level position. The specific difficulties in this stage are: a) how do we select from a number of talented but unprepared people, and b) how do we get the person we want to accept this position?

The Replacement Planning Stage

A somewhat more advanced process would be *replacement planning*, in which senior executives periodically review their top executives and those in the next-lower echelon and agree on two or three back-ups for each senior slot. The difference between replacement planning and staffing is that staffing is done for individual positions at the time they are vacant. Replacement is done on a regular time schedule, in advance of vacancies, for a large number of positions. It is often done subjectively, without establishing clear job descriptions (and related skills and experiences required). Because the criteria for selecting potential replacements are so subjective, and because back-ups are selected by a team of executives who have "grown up" in the company together, they may come to tacit agreement about the qualifications of candidates, and the agreement may never be tested against skill criteria that may be relevant but are not in the minds of the decision makers. As one CEO of a large manufacturing firm put it, "Our problem is not picking the people. The problem is that the same names keep showing up on every back-up list. The talent is so thin." In other words, not enough people have been developed to be ready to move into senior management. (And this comment came from the leader of an old "Theory Z" company, well known for strong management and a well established policy of promoting from within.) Thus, the replacement planning approach is simply an extension of the staffing approach, with more square or round pegs and holes to be matched up. The problem here, then, is likely to be a *shortage of executive talent.*

The Succession Planning Stage

The next logical step, then, is to move beyond replacement planning (where the focus is on filling future openings) to more of a conscious *succession planning* process, in which the focus is on both the future executive positions and the people who might be candidates for these positions. At the heart of most well developed succession systems is the *human-resource review session* (Friedman, 1985). In these reviews, the top executive group reviews managers above a certain level (usually upper-middle management) in terms of their current performance, future potential, developmental needs, and plans for addressing those needs. However, if the replacement planning process errs by focusing too much on specific jobs, the succession planning review process may put too much stress on the people and too little on the positions. In particular, insufficient thought may be given to *future* positions and how job demands and needed skills may shift over time.

Friedman (1985) has described how the succession planning process operates in two companies noted for excellent management (both general management and human resource management): General Electric and Honeywell. During the planned human resource review sessions, critical human resource issues are discussed by the top people in the corporation. Many CEO-hours per quarter (and hours of other top executives) are devoted to human resource planning. Particular attention is paid to the promotional and developmental needs and plans of subordinates. Written forms are used as a basis for discussion. And at GE, for each manager under review, that person's boss is held *accountable* for the implementation of the development plans agreed upon for that manager. Thus, there is both planning and follow-up action by senior executives, and the critical (and often neglected) link between planning and developmental action is successfully made.

Data Credibility. However, even in effective succession planning processes, problems arise in the area of development. For example, the head of executive development for a major automobile company speaks in positive terms (up to a point) of his company's succession system:

> Our procedures are as good as any. We have the annual management review sessions. We discuss potential and performance. We examine developmental needs and we agree on developmental plans. We establish accountability. The resulting forms look great.
>
> The only problem is that people don't pay any attention to them.

The reasons why these succession plans get so little attention, in this executive's opinion, is that these top executives, having come up the ranks through engineering or finance, are accustomed to working with quantitative, objective data. They are not comfortable with the more subjective evaluations of people that are contained in these management reviews, and thus the reviews tend to be discounted.

> Top management has to make the transition to a different measurement system, a different kind of data. It drives the engineers and financial people nuts.
>
> And, incidentally, this is the same problem they're having in making the transition to listening to customers. Customers may not always have a logical, rational reason for not liking a certain feature of a car. Their attitude may be quite subjective. But if it's clear that this car is rated poorly by lots of customers, we've got to listen to them.

*Uncertainty about Future Executive Skill Requirements.** In addition to a lack of confidence in the data about executive candidates, top management also often lacks confidence about the kinds of executive skills that the organization will require in the future. While their business planners may be telling them about new directions in which the company will have to move to be competitive in the future, top management may be uncomfortable basing too many executive decisions on this information. They are often willing to commit considerable financial and marketing resources to a strategic plan, but they often balk at, or simply fail to see, the possibility of committing major human resources (i.e., executive selection decisions) to the strategic plan. (This is especially a problem when the strategic planning data point to the selection of a person who is radically different from the current top management team, as we will discuss in the following section.) Further, drawing inferences from the business strategy about requisite future executive skills would serve to increase top management's uncertainty and anxiety. And under conditions of uncertainty and anxiety (and thus, probably, disagreement), when faced with a promotion decision critical to the future of the organization, top management will probably play it safe by selecting a "right type" executive (i.e., someone who resembles them).

In many organizations, senior human resource planners have attempted, without success, to obtain the business strategy information from top management which would be necessary in inferring future executive skill requirements. This situation occurred, for example, at AT&T after the divestiture, and the human resource planners were forced to develop their own conclusions about what the new AT&T executive should look like.

Selecting Dissimilar Types of Executives for the Future. The problem of data credibility is aggravated when top management consciously at-

---

* The author is indebted to Chris Argyris for pointing out this issue.

tempts to identify the skills executives will need in the future. This goes strongly against the grain, as executives, being human, normally tend to select successors in their own image. For example, in a classic study of a bank, Argyris (1954) found that top executives tended to systematically recruit and promote a "right type" of person, one similar to their own personal style. Rosabeth Moss Kanter (1977) refers to this process as "homosocial reproduction." Most senior executives are in the later years of middle adulthood, a time when they have a strong developmental need for generativity, to leave behind their own "fingerprints," a lasting contribution to future generations. What better way to achieve a sense of "industrial immortality" than to leave the corporation under the command of a younger version of yourself?

However, today's enlightened managers, informed by a strong consensus among influential management thinkers (e.g., Drucker, Naisbett, Peters and Waterman, Bennis and Nanus), realize that a manager with a different profile of skills and experience will be needed to lead the organization of the future: a good manager of people, a participative executive, an inspiring leader, more independent and entrepreneurial, a global thinker, etc. Elsewhere in this issue, Gupta (1986) also argues that it may be necessary sometimes to select executives who do not fit the present organization. It becomes extremely difficult for top management to have confidence that they are selecting successors with this new profile when there are no data they can trust. Before, when executives were selecting successors in their own image, the data were less important, since they could use their own intuition, a sense that "he's one of us." (And he usually was a he.) In one large company with a largely intuition-driven, very subjective succession system, the operative description of a high potential candidate was, "We feel good about him."

Summary of the Three Stages

A summary of the three stages in the development of succession systems is shown in Table I. The major problem with the staffing approach is that it is a one-shot, high-pressure activity where the concern is meeting an immediate crisis of succession. There is little opportunity for organizational learning and advance planning, or for learning by potential future candidates. The advantage, however, is that the crisis of a present opening gets the immediate attention of top management and thus their involvement in the process. Replacement planning focuses on the future and on a full set of positions, but it does not consider the developmental needs of candidates; in a sense, then, replacement planning is like an extension of the staffing approach, but with a multiposition, future-oriented perspective. Succession planning, on the other hand, takes into account the requirements of future positions and the development needs of candidates for these positions. Criteria are more

Table I.   A Summary of Three Stages in the Evolution of Succession Systems.

	Stage 1: One-position Staffing	Stage 2: Replacement Planning	Stage 3: Succession Planning
Time Frame	present	future	future
Number of Executive Positions Considered	one	many	many
Focus on Position Requirements	high	high	high
Focus on Candidates' Learning Requirements	low	low	high
Most Frequently-used Type of Data Employed	subjective	subjective	objective
Attention of Top Management	extremely high	variable	variable

likely to be objective because the process is more comprehensive than replacement planning or staffing. However, because of the future orientation of both replacement planning and succession planning, there may be more variability in top management's attention to these processes.

Strategic Development Planning

To avoid the pitfalls of the one-shot staffing approach, the replacement planning approach, and the succession planning approach, a new method is required: *strategic development planning* (Hall, 1984), the linking of strategic organizational objectives to future executive job requirements. Here the focus is on the necessary redesign of the executive positions of the future as demanded by business objectives, as well as on the identification and development of executive candidates with the necessary skills to fit these future position profiles. The person *and* the position are both viewed as changing over time in ways that are not always predictable. Thus, the capacities for continual *learning* and *adaptability* (in both the organization and the executive) are needed in the succession process.

PROBLEMS IN LINKING LEARNING TO SUCCESSION

The complexity of succession processes varies greatly from company to company. It ranges from General Motor's yearly appraisal of its top 5000 managers, with predictions about where they will be in five years and at the end of their careers, to Dana Corp.'s system, which merely rotates managers "and sees how they do." As one Dana official said, "it's not very exotic or carefully planned" (*Wall Street Journal*, 1985).

Typically, though, management reviews are conducted once a year and are done by the company's top executives, assisted by senior human resource executives. The initial step is identifying the top 10 or 15 percent of management jobs in the organization that are most critical. Then, the knowledge, skills, and abilities necessary to perform well in each of these jobs are determined. Then, a pool of back-up candidates (usually one to four) is identified. Finally, a developmental or learning plan for each of these candidates is established, to insure that they will have sufficient education, skill, and experience to fill the positions for which they are being prepared.

The review process, then, is critical in identifying the learning needs of the candidate. Walter Mahler, an expert in succession planning, has described the effectiveness of the management review component in rather gloomy terms:

> Reviews have been with us for decades. We have been amazed to discover that the full potential of reviews have seldom been realized. A delightful variety of ways have been used to handicap the review process. (Mahler, 1982)

Mahler cites numerous pitfalls in the review process which can be responsible for ineffectiveness. The most important are: lack of interest and involvement by the CEO; reviews are done, but results do not occur; the review process is viewed by line management as the responsibility of the human resource function; the process is too complex; there is insufficient preparation for the reviews; and there is inadequate follow-through on action plans coming out of the reviews. Thus, the executive learning that was proposed in the review may simply never occur.

Let us consider some of the important problems which can lead to these learning failures.

1. Succession Divorced from Strategy

Often the dimensions on which managers are reviewed are not systematically derived from the basic strategic mission and goals of the organization. Instead, they are often "boy or girl scout" qualities that are implicitly accepted by top management as important attributes of future executives: decisiveness, communication skills, problem solving, interpersonal skills, effort and commitment, etc. Some of these dimensions may, in fact, be those the organization will need in the future to achieve its objectives, but often this question is not addressed. Often the mission and goals are not specific enough to be related to executive skill requirements and, as we said earlier, top management may feel too uncertain about future business projections to use them as a basis for selecting new types of executives. Or it may simply not occur to top management to consider the business strategy in making executive staffing decisions.

Often the sheer volume of reviews that must be performed drives out any longer-term considerations of what sort of executive the organization is trying to grow. Other factors which may work against longer-term thinking are the lack of rewards for long-term development and the difficulty in measuring long-term learning outcomes.

2. Homosocial Reproduction

There are several issues which arise from having the CEO and immediate reports conduct the annual reviews. The first is the danger of what Rosabeth Kanter (1977) has called "homosocial reproduction." This is the tendency of a group of senior executives to try (often unconsciously) to perpetuate the organization's future leadership in their own images; i.e., to choose successors who are very much like themselves. We know from research on selection that a common rating error is for an evaluator to rate more highly than those people who are like him- or herself (Schneider and Schmitt, 1986). Argyris (1985) has described how a "group think" effect can develop through the creation of defensive, self-sealing routines in executive group decision-making.

Training of raters can be an effective way to reduce this similarity bias, but it is unlikely that a human resource professional would attempt to provide formal training to the CEO and the senior executive group. Solid data on performance and potential, in the form of assessment ratings, performance appraisals, and boss evaluations can also help reduce this bias. The fact that there are multiple raters in a group review process also helps reduce rater bias. However, as the executive education manager quoted earlier in this paper indicated, many executives came up through engineering or finance and simply do not trust the "soft" data which result from human resource evaluation processes. Thus, the executives often tend to over-rely on their answer to the question, "Do we feel good about this person?"

3. Over-stress on Identification; Under-stress on Development

In many cases the top executive review group sees its primary task as being the identification of high potential candidates. There is a tendency for them to think (again perhaps subconciously) that development and learning will take care of themselves. The main thing is to get the right person on track for that key position. This problem can result from the scarcity of time among these top executives who are doing the ratings. When time gets tight, identification comes first (in the logical order of the process, as well as in psychological priority) and gets the most attention, driving out time for working on development plans. And what time is spent on development tends to be devoted to task learning rather than personal learning. Another contributing factor here is that the human resource staff who prepare the paperwork for the review put most of their time in on presenting the evaluation data, because those are available and relatively quantitative. Not only do the executive reviewers not place priority on development, but they are not experts on development (particularly on personal learning), so both the ability and the motivation to produce good learning plans are lacking.

4. Insufficient Follow-Up on Development Activities

In many organizations, the review process effectively stops at the end of the meeting of the senior executive group. The results of the review are committed to paper, and there is often little monitoring of the development plans. As Friedman (1986) says elsewhere in this issue, executive development is the "backbone" of succession systems. One simple way to promote development is General Electric's process of holding a particular executive *accountable* for the implementation of the development plans of his or her subordinates under review. For example, Friedman (1986) described how one CEO, who based 10 percent of his executives' bonus on their plans for subordinate development, was able to get their attention focused on development. Another problem here can be when the human resource function is responsible for follow-up; if the line organization is not the locus of accountability, it will not happen.

5. Too Little Candidate Involvement

Another problem of having top management conduct the reviews is that they are then treated as confidential corporate property. No one outside this group, especially not the candidate, receives any information about the outcomes of the process. For example, at Citicorp, an organization known for its excellent succession process, pictures of key position incumbents and their backup candidates are kept on a board covered by locked doors in the board room. Only two people have keys to these doors, the CEO and the head of the review process (Saklad, 1976).

The problem with low candidate involvement is that the organization has little information about the person's willingness to assume the position or to engage in the developmental actions which are being planned for him or her. And then if he or she turns the position down, a crisis occurs. The solution here is fairly simple: incorporate information about the candidate's career plans and goals (from his or her own career planning process) along with other inputs to the review process. It is striking, however, how many companies do not include good information from the candidate in the review process. Succession planning and career planning are often two totally separate processes in many organizations (Hall, 1986).

6. Antidevelopmental Consequences of Succession Planning

Not only does a formal succession planning process not facilitate development for the executive, but *in many cases a succession planning process actively inhibits executive learning.* This can happen in several ways. First, if the succession process is known throughout the organization and if lower-level managers are aware of a potential assessment process, there is often a sense that certain assignments are on the "fast track." If a person perceives that he or she is on a fast track (one is rarely told), the attitude this creates is one of playing it safe: "don't screw up." The important thing is having that critical job, getting one's ticket punched; performance in the job is secondary. So the last thing the person would do is take a risk, assume more challenge and responsibility, and attempt to learn something new. The person avoids activities that could lead to new learning.

Another learning casualty of typical succession processes is the individual who realizes that he or she is not on the fast track. This realization understandably leads to reduced motivation and commitment. And this group of not-fast-track "solid citizens" most probably amounts to 85 to 90 percent of the managers in the organization! This group is the backbone of the organization.

Thus, we often end up with no one feeling truly developed by the succession process. The high potentials are unwilling to risk learning, and the solid citizens are unmotivated to do so.

Another way the process frustrates learning objectives is that the high potential person knows that he or she will be on a given assignment for a short period of time, because of the high job mobility of fast track people. This knowledge leads to a stress on short-term results, the desire to make a "quick hit" to get a good performance rating. This means that investments in longer-term activities such as learning new skills or engaging in personal learning are not rewarded activities. And even if a person did initiate some longer-term activities, he or she would not be able to see the results. (There are a number of other negative consequences of fast track systems discussed in Thompson et al., 1985).

7. Executive Immaturity and Succession

The result of some succession planning process is often low self-control and passivity on the part of the executive candidate. As Argyris (1957) described years ago, formal organizational controls can create in the individual conditions such as passivity, loss of self-control, short time perspective, and psychological failure. Argyris referred to these personal qualities as indicators of developmental immaturity. These qualities of immaturity are precisely those which are fostered by many succession planning systems. The longer in life the executive feels that the organization is plotting a career path for him or her, the longer that person will go without assuming personal responsibility for his or her career. And assuming responsibility for oneself is an essential element in developmental maturity. Thus, we have the ironic situation in which a 52-year old vice president who is in the running for his company's CEO slot is less in control of his life than a 35 year old engineer who knows, as a result of conscious career planning, that she wants to spend the rest of her career in technical work. And this situation is aggravated by the fact that the executive's success, power, and isolation tend to cut him or her off from any feedback or criticism that might increase his or her awareness of this loss of control.

WHAT IS EXECUTIVE LEARNING?

There are two types of learning which are necessary as an executive develops (Hall, 1976). The first, which is that most generally associated with executive development, is *task learning:* improving the knowledge, skills, and abilities necessary to perform higher level jobs effectively. The second, rarely discussed in the succession and development literatures, is *personal learning:* the mastery of the socio-emotional tasks associated with the person's stage in life. Most of the writings in the succession literature ignore this facet of learning, thus completely overlooking the fact that executives are adults who have to "grow up" just like any other human being.

More specifically, these two types of learning relate to the four dimensions of career growth and effectiveness: performance, adaptability, attitudes, and identity (Hall, 1976). Performance and adaptability refer to short-term and long-term facets of task mastery, respectively. Attitudes and identity deal with, respectively, short-term and long-term facets of socio-emotional mastery. These four dimensions of career effectiveness are displayed in Table II. We would hypothesize that the more a succession system facilitates all four dimensions of career growth, the more effective that system will be. Our discussion of executive learning will be organized around the matrix in Table II.

Task Learning

Not only is most work on executive development based upon the assumption that "development" means task learning, but, further, task learning is generally defined in terms of the shorter-term issues of im-

Table II.   Task and Personal Learning Dimensions in Career Effectiveness.

	Task Learning	Personal Learning
Short Term	Improving *performance*-related knowledge, skills and abilities	Resolving issues regarding *attitudes* toward career and personal life.
Long Term	Improving *adaptability*	Developing and extending *identity*

proving performance capability. The longer-term issues of enhancing adaptive abilities have rarely been discussed.

As organizations increasingly face discontinuous change, there is more need for radical transformation. Take, as an example, AT&T. It has undergone perhaps the most major organizational change in business history as a result of the 1984 divestiture (Campbell and Moses, 1986). As the company deals with the need to be more flexible and adaptive, defending its old markets (telecommunications) from new deregulated competitors and entering new ones (information) against "heavy hitters" like IBM, it strongly needs executives who are similarly flexible and adaptive. How can an organization with a long history of promotion from within and the resulting senior executive cadre with "Bell-shaped heads" (to quote the AT&T vernacular) suddenly transform its up-and-coming executives into a more flexible group with a new profile of skills?

The strong company loyalty which AT&T's promotion from within system has bred over the years, through a process of career-long socialization which had been a great strength of the old Bell System, has now become an obstacle to executive learning and adaptation, and thus to corporate adaptation. Thus, the major need in the area of task learning is along the longer-term process of adaptability. (Short term task needs, such as new skills and abilities, are more easily dealt with through specific training programs and through superior–subordinate performance coaching.)

One lesson from the AT&T experience seems to be that there are two facets of loyalty. One is loyalty to the basic mission and goals (e.g., high-quality service) of the organization, and this form of commitment is *not* an obstacle to flexibility and adaptation. In fact, it provides motivation for the person to help the organization respond to new environmental conditions. The other type of loyalty can be an attachment to specific methods (policies and procedures) for attaining end-result goals; this type of attachment can produce resistance to change. Thus, organizational socialization attempts should focus on developing consensus and commitment on end results and not on specific policies and procedures.

Enhancing adaptability. What enables a person to adapt to new methods and approaches after 20 or 30 years of working in another way? The author has proposed a model of midcareer change which deals with the issue of the *career routine* that develops as the person becomes established in a career field (Hall, 1986). This routine is initially functional in that it enables the person to perform at a high level without a great deal of conscious thought, at least as far as most everyday task activities are concerned. By having the routine portion of one's work become scripted or programmed in this way, it frees up the person's creative resources for nonroutine activities. The routine also enables the person to work at a high performance level with a reduced level of total effort, which makes it possible to put more energy into one's personal and family life; and this move toward balance between work and personal life is a major developmental task of the person in midlife. (Let us not forget that most executives are, in fact, *persons in midlife*.) Thus, as the person is moving into the establishment stage of the career, the creation of career routines, the elimination of surprise (Louis, 1980), is a major developmental activity in achieving mastery in the career.

Ironically, what leads to success in one career stage can cause stagnation and failure in the next. Routine is functional up to a certain point, but if *all* of a person's activities become scripted, there is no room for innovation. If the person's early success is too strongly reinforced and scripted, the risk of change will seem greater than it would for the person who was less successful earlier. And if the person's early career was spent in one specialized area or function, this would make it harder to adapt to a new specialty, a new function, or a new technology. The larger and stronger the career routine becomes, the more difficult adaptation is. *Thus, we often see a conflict between the short term and long term task dimensions: the more successful the person's present performance is, the more difficult future adaptability will be.* And, to make matters worse, the higher an executive is in an organization, the more his or her power inhibits his receiving feedback and helpful criticism from other people (Kaplan et al., 1985). Thus, career success impedes learning.

The issue, then, is what facilitates "routine busting" for established executives? A number of triggering factors are proposed. These are influences in the organization, task, or person which operate as either push or pull factors. That is, they either put pressure on the person to change (e.g., new technology), or they make it easier or more attractive to change (e.g., new attractive promotion in a new area). These factors are illustrated in Figure 1. Kaplan (1985) argues that a similar set of influences lead an executive to engage in self-criticism and self-examination and also lead him or her to receive unsolicited criticism; if the executive accepts the criticism, the next step would be to attempt to change.

What is adaptability? The trigger events and personality variables which impact on the career routine in Figure 1 are the ingredients contributing to a person's overall level of adaptability. The more the person's work or personal environment provides the trigger listed (e.g., rewards for

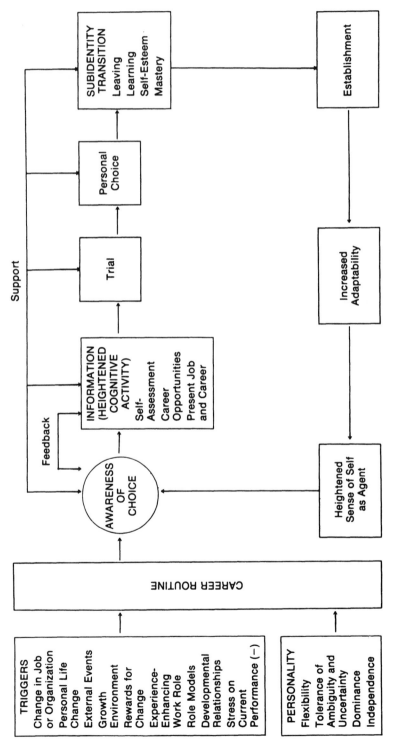

Figure 1.   Factors in career routine change.

change, role models of adaptable people) the greater the adaptability would be. The one negative here would be stress on current performance, which would work against longer-term development.

A cluster of personality factors combine to make a person more open to change: flexibility, tolerance of ambiguity and change, dominance (representing an aspect of positive self-esteem or personality "hardiness"), and independence. Research and practice at AT&T has shown that these personal qualities can be measured in assessment centers. This AT&T work also shows that adaptability will be a critical personality attribute of future executives in that organization.

Once the career routine is busted, the person is then motivated to explore new areas of career task activity. Next, he or she tries out a new activity. This trial activity could be as simple as serving on a corporate task force related to the new area, or it could be making the move to a totally new type of work. Feedback and support are strongly needed to facilitate these exploratory and trial activities. If the person performs well in this new task activity, this success will probably alter his or her sense of identity, as the career identity will now contain some important new task-related knowledge, skills, and abilities.

Successful activity in a new task area will probably feed back to affect the person's motivation to engage in future career exploration and change. Thus, a successful experience with career change will probably increase the person's general level of career adaptability. This relationship could be stated in proposition form:

P1: A person who has had a successful experience with career change will have higher adaptability than a person who has not experienced career change (i.e., who has stayed within one area of task activity).

P2: A person who has had a successful experience with career change will have a higher level of career adaptability than a person with a less successful career change experience.

This second proposition is debatable. It could be that a person who had an unsuccessful career change experience might learn even more from it than a more successful change, especially if the failure led to eventual success. A critical factor here would probably be the person's style of dealing with failure. If the person tried to deny it or if their self-esteem were so weak that they were crushed by failure, they would probably be more resistant to change in the future. On the other hand, if he were willing to examine and learn from failure, he would be more likely to convert it to later success, and thus greater adaptability.

The importance of adaptability was demonstrated in a study of "derailed" executives by McCall and Lombardo (1983). They found that derailed executives had enjoyed a series of successes, but these successes were usually in similar situations. They had done the same type of thing (e.g., turn troubled businesses around) several times over. The successful executives (the "arrivers"), on the other hand, had had more *diversity* in their successes. Perhaps they had started up a new business successfully, then managed a large complex project, and then served in a key staff role. Thus, the more changes they had had in their career, the more adaptive these executives were. And the more adaptive they were, the more success they experienced. These findings are also consistent with the work of Bartunek and Louis (1985), who found that the strongest correlate of development (as measured by cognitive complexity) for experienced people entering a new organizational environment was task variety. Thus, diverse, varied experience appears to be a major influence on a person's adaptability.

Types of Task Learning. Let us now switch to another issue: the type of task learning involved. A classic article by Katz (1974) identifies three types of managerial task activity and three concomitant skills a manager needs. At lower organizational levels, technical skills are most important, as supervisors are directly responsible for getting the main work of the organization done: the product out the door or the services delivered to the customer. At middle levels, interpersonal skills become more important, as a high degree of coordination with other managers and supervisors is required. At senior levels, conceptual skills become especially important, as the executive must scan and deal with a complex environment, analyze strategic issues, and engage in long-term planning. In an update of the original article, Katz acknowledged that technical skills were now more important at senior levels than he originally thought they were; an executive must know something about the basics of his or her business. Being simply a good general manager is not enough.

Thus, at the senior executive level, the person would have been expected to have mastered technical and interpersonal skills. The major new task learning for senior executives would be expected to be conceptual skills. In propositional form:

P3: The major type of learning for senior executives should be conceptual skills as opposed to technical and interpersonal skills.

Personal Learning

Returning to the dimensions of learning in Table II, we now focus on the short term issues of attitudes toward career (*vis-a-vis* personal life) and the longer term process of developing one's sense of identity.

Career and Life Attitudes. A major deficiency in the work on executive development has been the lack of attention to the fact that executives are people in midlife who face all of the developmental life tasks which are normally associated with that life stage (Levinson et al., 1978). A person in their 40s or 50s must deal with feelings about aging, the loss of parents, the maturing of children, physiological change, illnesses, and getting better balance between energy invested in work vs. energy invested in personal involvements. Generativity is a major concern at this stage of life: the desire to see one's work and contributions passed on to future generations.

For many managers, this is a period when their career attainments and promotions begin to level off and plateau (Hall, 1986). While there are many problems associated with plateauing (Hall, 1985), one advantage is that it does free the person up to invest more energy in other spheres of his or her life. However, the executive who is a candidate for still higher positions under a succession plan does not have the "luxury" of plateauing; there is no extra energy for home and family. In fact, the person who is potentially about to make the critical transition from middle to senior management has probably never worked harder or experienced more career stress than he or she does right now. More and more the person becomes "married" to the organization. The hours get longer, the travel increases, business socializing increases, symbolic and figurehead duties become more frequent, and the spouse (if there is one) is called upon more and more to be at the executive's side. Lee Iacocca (1984, reviewed in this issue) describes in detail how this absorptive process worked at higher executive levels at Ford and Chrysler.

The increased demands of career on personal life at the executive level are aggravated by the fact that the executive is expected to accept these organizational commitments eagerly and cheerfully. It is not socially desirable to see these as areas of conflict (at least at work), so they are not discussable. And this nondiscussability leads to even more stress.

Thus, executive learning should include the opportunity to discuss and explore one's attitudes toward career and personal life. More specifically, the potential senior executive should have an opportunity to do a self-assessment of his or her own needs, interests, skills, and life priorities in relation to the demands and rewards of possible higher-level executive positions to see how well he or she would fit in those positions. This self-assessment should play a major role in determining whether or not the person will remain a high potential candidate. Such a self-assessment would increase the person's fit in higher positions.

P4: A succession system that includes a careful self-assessment by high-potential executive candidates will result in better future career fits than a succession system in which self-assessment is not included.

Identity. This issue of at once maintaining individuality in the context of a highly involving relationship with the organization is the highest (fifth) level of development, according to Robert Kegan (1982). The person has already gone through earlier stages such as "imperial" (self-preoccupation), "interpersonal" (defining self through one's relationships), and "institutional" (self-definitive through task and organizational involvement). The person must now resolve what it means to be a separate person within the context of being a senior representative of the organization. Kegan calls this the "interindividual" stage. This stage requires growing out of a preoccupation with one's career and relationships (at work and in personal life) and becoming *inter*dependent, being truly one's own person, while being part of a highly involving, committed relationship. For a senior executive, this means going from being a good "organization person" and team player, to being a self-directed, self-aware organizational leader.

One way the executive can do this "identity work" is through a process of self-observation and self-reflection. One method of doing this would be a process of personal therapy. This is becoming more acceptable to more people in contemporary society. An alternative is what Kegan calls "natural therapies." These are experiences which create the conditions for important personal learning in naturally-occurring settings. Kegan discusses "holding environments," where support is provided, immediate pressures are removed, and the person feels psychologically free to engage in identity exploration.

Argyris (1982) found that personal therapy and identity clarification occur when executives decide or are asked to produce *rare events* in their organization. In trying to thus define organizational identity (by identifying and creating exceptions to that identity), they are thus also examining personal identity as well, by reflecting upon their feelings and reactions to this risk-taking process.

Another approach to self-reflection is that of Argyris and Schön (1974). They describe two models of learning. Model I is single loop learning, in which the person receives feedback on performance and can thus be self-correcting in relation to his or her present goals and objectives. However, a person operating in a Model I mode does not question those goals or the basic process in which he or she is engaged. This is a process of single loop learning; it is constrained by the basic assumptions with which the person started.

In contrast, Model II, or double loop, learning not only permits feedback on performance, but also permits an examination of the basic assumptions, values, and goals which are guiding the person's behavior. Model II not only corrects one's aim toward the target, it also lets the person question why he or she is aiming at the target. Model II permits basic assumptions and "undiscussable" norms to become discussable and open for examination and possible revision. Most traditional executive development experiences are consistent with Model I, in that they do not encourage participants to examine their own behavior in relation to the personal values and assumptions which guide that behavior.

The self-reflective learning of Model II is consistent with what Bennis and Nanus (1985) describe as the effective executive's ability to: learn in an organizational context, concentrate on the key elements in the organizational environment, and use the organization as a medium for learning. Their successful executives possess a set of skills which have what Donald Michael calls "the new competence":

1. Acknowledging and sharing uncertainty
2. Embracing error
3. Responding to the future
4. Becoming interpersonally competent (i.e., listening, nurturing, coping with value conflicts, etc.)
5. Gaining self knowledge (Donald Michael, cited by Bennis and Nanus, 1985, p. 189)

Argyris and Schön argue that for organizations to be more adaptive to the demands of their environments, it is necessary for organizational leaders to become capable of this higher-order, self-reflective, Model II learning. For a person to be able to learn the Model II process, it would appear that the basic identity of the executive would have to become subject to self-examination. This would require opportunities to inquire about one's basic goals and values and to consider the extent to which one is actually behaving in ways that are consistent with those goals and values.

It sounds like a straightforward process to examine values in relation to behavior, but in practice it is a very complex learning process, as Argyris and Schön describe the seminars in which they encourage this learning to take place. It involves a complex set of iterations of initially stating values, then testing them against one's behavior, identifying inconsistencies, revising one's view of one's values, changing behavior, and reinforcing new action patterns. This process is quite different from most of what is called "executive development" in contemporary organizations, in that the latter is typically aimed at the learning of new task skills and concepts rather than personal learning.

To summarize, then, personal learning involves the self-reflective process of examining and possibly changing one's attitudes and identity. Here the focus is the person, not a performance task. A different learning technology is necessary for personal learning than for task learning, as we will see in the following section.

METHODS FOR EXECUTIVE TASK AND PERSONAL LEARNING

In an earlier paper, the author discussed different methods of learning that were appropriate for the four different dimensions of career effectiveness (performance, attitudes, adaptability, and identity) (Hall, 1984).

The first method is *receptive,** which involves didactic activities, such as classroom lectures, discussion, and reading to alter thoughts and ideas, where the learner is basically passive. The second is *active*, which involves creating situations requiring action by the person; this active behavior of the person then creates learning. And the third approach is *environmental*, which consists of interventions aimed at altering the work environment of the individual to produce learning.

I will argue that receptive approaches are overused in executive education, that environmental methods are misused, and that behavioral methods are underused. I will further argue that a balance among these methods is needed, and that the different methods must be better integrated.

My point about receptive methods may not need much elaboration. In the developmental action plans from many succession planning processes, the recommendations often include specific courses or educational programs which the high potential candidates would attend (e.g., the Harvard Advanced Management Program, or an in-house executive development program). However, receptive methods are probably best suited for conveying basic information (facts, theories, etc.) to improve the person's technical or conceptual skills to improve along the performance dimension. Receptive methods are not very effective in improving interpersonal performance skills, or for the other three career effectiveness dimensions: attitudes, adaptability, and identity. *However, in many contemporary organizations, executive development in synonymous with formal receptive classroom teaching methods.*

Why are receptive methods overused? Because they are easy to implement. It is relatively simple to design and deliver a new two-week executive program for all managers at a certain level of the organization. It is even easier to send a certain number of high-potential people off to a university summer program. And if previous generations of executives have gone through certain methods, they are likely to feel that future leaders should go through the same process. In the process of homosocial reproduction (choosing successors in their own images), incumbent leaders also want those successors to have had similar development experiences.

Now, what about environmental methods? These involve putting the person in certain environments which are intended to generate certain learnings. Examples would be job rotation, temporary assignments, task force assignments, employee exchanges, and job and organization redesign. In many cases, a development plan in a succession planning process would include a "broadening" or "developmental" assignment in

---

* These terms have been revised from the 1984 paper. The term "receptive" has replaced "cognitive," since new forms of learning can be behavioral and cognitive (Argyris, 1982). "Active" is used in place of behavioral to clarify the focus on personal activity and involvement.

another department or division, a temporary assignment, a stint on a certain corporate committee, or involvement in a civic or charitable organization. In many cases the particular skills or personal attributes which would be developed by these assignments are not well thought out; there may just be a feeling that the experience would be "good" for the person, or the assignment may be a corporate "ticket" that needs to be punched. Thus, it appears that environmental methods have not been overused; they have simply been inappropriately used. In fact, they contain great potential for improved utilization.

Active methods, on the other hand, have been underutilized. These are consciously designed activities which are devised with certain personal development objectives in mind. Examples would be planned socialization experiences, developmental assessment centers, career and personal counseling, behavior modeling, role playing, outplacement, apprenticeships, and on-the-job learning assignments. A good active learning task would be combination of cognitive and environmental methods in that it could be an experimental application of a particular method or concept, which the person consciously applies in a real situation. For task learning, there is nothing so potent as trying to practice a new method oneself; for example, it is difficult to imagine learning to play golf just by hearing classroom lectures on the subject. Similarly for personal learning, the best way to examine one's attitudes and identity would be by seeing how they are reflected in one's actual behavior. And certainly when it came to *changing* attitudes and identity, these changes could be confirmed only through their manifestations in actual behavior (i.e., by using active methods).

In addition to needing more use of active methods in executive learning, we also need better integration of the different methods. Research on obsolescence has shown that formal classroom training (or retraining) methods are not especially effective as midcareer learning methods all by themselves. However, when classroom activities are linked to specific job needs for new learning, these cognitive methods can be effective (Hall, 1976). In other words, if an executive needs to do strategic planning in a new assignment, then formal classes on that topic will produce good learning, since the executive has a clear *need to learn* and an *opportunity to apply* that learning. However, giving a new management trainee a formal class on strategic planning would probably be experienced as purely academic, and there may be little knowledge retention.

Integrating these different learning methods to facilitate personal learning would be more complex than the task learning example in the preceding paragraph. Some cognitive input would be necessary on adult development stages, work vs. family issues, perhaps some philosophy, ethics, and other readings related to values and personal growth. Active behavior would have to be designed to help the person examine his or her own activities, lifestyle, and work environment, as well as possible alternative activities, lifestyle, and work environments. And work assignments and "take home" course assignments would be needed to take these new learnings into the everyday work environment.

Accomplishing this learning integration would involve cooperation between people responsible for formal executive (classroom) development functions (e.g., General Electric's Crotonville facility), staff people responsible for succession planning, and line executives who supervise the high potential candidates. *This tripartite sharing of responsibility between executive educators, succession planners, and line executives is the crux of a more effective executive learning process.*

The organizational commitment and resources to encourage this kind of cooperation are most likely to be found in what Bennis and Nanus (1985) call a "learning organization."

> Organizational learning is the process by which an organization obtains and uses new knowledge, tools, behavior, and values. It happens at all levels in the organization, among individuals and groups, as well as system-wide. Individuals learn as part of their daily activities, particularly as they interact with each other and the outside world. Groups learn as their members cooperate to accomplish common goals. The entire system learns as it obtains feedback from the environment and anticipates further changes. At all levels, newly learned knowledge is translated into new goals, procedures, expectations, role structures, and measures of success. (Bennis and Nanus, 1985, p. 191).

The more learning is built in to the culture of the organization, the more likely it is that the kinds of task and personal executive learning we have been discussing will take place.

Of all the qualities necessary for executive success, the capacity for personal learning is probably the most important. Personal learning is a "meta-skill." If the executive has learned how he or she learns (Model II), then he or she has acquired the capacity to master more specific tasks. And, in fact, in their study of executive leaders, Bennis and Nanus (1985) found what we are calling personal learning to be their most prized personal quality:

> When we asked our 90 leaders about the personal qualities they needed to run their organizations, they never mentioned charisma, or dressing for success, or time management, or any of the other glib formulas that pass for wisdom in the popular press. Instead, they talked about persistence and self-knowledge; about willingness to take risks and accept losses; about commitment, consistency, and challenge. But, above all, they talked about [personal] learning. (Bennis and Nanus, 1985, pp. 187–188)

So why does not executive learning occur more frequently as part and parcel of formal succession planning processes? We will now consider some of the ways of linking learning to succession.

WHAT TO DO?

How can these learning problems be addressed? Let us conclude with some suggestions for strengthening the link between succession processes, individual executive learning, and business strategy.

1. Make Executive Learning Strategic

Elsewhere (Hall, 1984), the author has discussed the process of strategic human resource development, "the identification of needed skills and active management of employee learning for the long-range future in relation to explicit corporate and business strategies" (p. 159). To do this at the executive learning level would require a conscious examination of the corporate strategy for the future and then a logical derivation of the necessary skills and personal learnings that will be necessary for future executives to be able to implement this strategy.

This means doing a *future job analysis* for key executive positions. Executive job demands will have to be derived from the objectives identified in the firm's strategic planning process. Furthermore, it will be necessary to have human resource professionals who specialize in executive job analysis do much of this work, in consultation with senior management. This task cannot be the responsibility of top management alone, as they lack the necessary analytic skills. Thinking through this link between the organization's basic objectives and the needed future top executive skills is the core of strategic succession planning. Determining ways to identify and develop candidates with the needed qualities are secondary in importance to this strategic first step. One requirement for improving this link is with a strong, professional succession staff (Friedman, 1986).

2. Up the Ante on Executive Learning

To "grow" these strategically necessary qualities in candidates, it will be necessary to find ways to increase the priority and preparation of development plans. The CEO should ask for two or three alternative development plans for each candidate and then lead a discussion of the relative merits of each, before settling on one course of action. The human resource staff could be asked to prepare an *executive guide to development activities* that would help the thinking of the top group when it comes time to set development plans. A high-level corporate task force could be created to design new ways of learning, dealing explicitly with the different learning needs for task learning and personal learning. Personal learning (attitudes and identity) should be given an explicit "blessing" by the CEO, in much the same way James Renier has done at Honeywell (Renier, 1985).

Part of what is needed here is sheer *time* from the CEO and top management. Careful executive reviews which adequately cover both assessment and development take many weeks of scarce executive time each year. Yet these reviews and their follow-up activities are key to the success of the process (Friedman, 1986). As one specific way to provide time for executive learning, Bank of America has a policy that every manager at every level receive 40 hours of training per year (Beck, 1985).

3. Encourage Active Learning for Executives

As we have said before, executives are a disadvantaged group when it comes to personal control and life planning. While they are in positions of great organizational power, their personal lives are controlled more by the needs of the organization than are the lives of their subordinates. And they generally have had little say in the decisions that have affected their careers. Many companies (e.g., Citicorp), in fact, use the term "corporate property" to describe their highest potential managers, a term which captures this flavor of organizational control. Fifty percent of Friedman's (1984) samples of 235 companies reported they had a variant of the "corporate property" policy. As a result, executives often experience what Korman and Korman (1980) found to be a state of career success and personal failure (failed marriages, alienated children, few close friends, etc.).

To contribute to a more psychologically healthy senior executive group, candidates for these positions should be encouraged and supported in various processes of personal learning. One way would be executive career planning. This would entail individually tailored self-assessment and personal planning activities provided by external counselors or consultants. This would be too confidential to be done by internal human resource staff. This planning could be provided as another executive benefit, much like financial planning assistance or medical benefits.

Another method would be by incorporating examination of work and family issues in executive development courses. Some of these activities could involve spouses, in much the same way as some companies invite spouses to attend social events during executive programs. Some innovative companies, such as Eli Lilly, are beginning to incorporate work/family issues into management education activities. As the number of two-career couples increases in most companies, the pressures to take family issues into consideration will grow correspondingly.

Another way to promote personal learning in executive seminars would be a careful examination of their own decision-making processes, as individuals and as a group. Argyris (1985) describes how strategic action can be improved by having executives generate their own cases of decision-making routines, including a "double entry" listing of what actually happened and what the executive was thinking or feeling at the time. By analyzing and discussing their own cases, the executives experience important personal learning about how their own assumptions create self-defeating behavior. The seminar also gives them the opportunity to experiment with new, more effective behavior. This use of self-generated, written cases involving the executive's own behavior is at once a powerful yet relatively nonthreatening method of promoting self-reflection and feedback from others.

In one consulting firm which was helping clients with strategic planning, Argyris (1986) found that teams of consultants could learn in a two-day seminar, through written examinations of their own case data, how to analyze and reduce defensive decision-making loops. They then found that not only did it make their own decision process more effective, but it was a method they found they could in turn use to help clients reduce "noise" and improve creative quality in their own decision-making.

A related activity is "action learning," in which a person or team is assigned a real organizational problem to solve as part of a formal classroom training experience. The participants are also given time at work to spend on this action project. This requires that the classroom activities be relevant to current corporate needs, and it builds in a connection between the classroom and the executive's work environment. This method was pioneered at General Electric Company in the United Kingdom (Casey and Pearce, 1977) and is now being adopted in the United States.

Experiential learning, such as the Center for Creative Leadership's "Looking Glass," is another powerful yet safe way for executives to get information on their own behavior. As Kaplan et al. (1985) have shown, executives tend to avoid personal learning, but three factors facilitate such learning: 1) setbacks, failures, and crisis, 2) external intervention, and 3) legitimate and available resources for self-development. The more the organization can make resources available *and* legitimate (a very important consideration), the less likelihood would there be of the first two factors arising.

4. Design Learning Seminars for Corporate Officers

To help establish and reinforce the importance of executive learning and make it part of the corporate culture, a specific early step would be the creation of *special seminars for corporate officers*. (In most firms, executive development programs cover a range of lower- and middle-level managers, but officers are rarely included. The assumption is that they are "already developed.") These seminars would be two- or three-day workshops where the top 50 or 100 people in the organization would meet in small groups of around 20 to discuss their roles, and actions they need to take to best support the strategic direction of the organization. Bolt (1985) discusses specific ways various companies (e.g., General Foods, Motorola, Xerox) have integrated corporate strategy into senior executive development activities. These seminars should *not* include the CEO, except perhaps in a wrap-up at the end to discuss the group's ideas on future actions. An important part of the learning agenda would be to help the officers become more effective as a group, in working with each other and with the CEO. A major pharmaceutical company is now planning a series of these "senior management conferences," as they term them, for the top 60 executives in the organization.

5. Integrate Succession and Career Planning; Involve the Candidate

This is perhaps the greatest need of all. We have two excellent systems in most organizations (succession planning and career planning), yet they often are housed in different parts of the organization and are totally independent of each other. It would be relatively easy to incorporate information on the candidate's interests, goals, and willingness to make various kinds of job moves into the succession planning process. This way, when it came time to make a certain move, top management would know in advance that the person would be ready and willing to go. A step in this direction in some firms is the addition to announcements of executive vacancies information about developmental opportunities which the job provides. This gives learning more prominence and also helps relate the opening to the individual's own career objectives.

6. Eliminate Fast Tracks; Create Developmental Environments and Candidate Pools

It is difficult to predict which individuals will be successful years into the future. And when we attempt to do so, we get into the negative unintended consequences of the fast track described earlier. So we should put our developmental eggs in many baskets. We should focus on developing *pools* of management candidates, rather than individual crown princes and princesses. *Rather than selecting high potential candidates first and then developing them, we are more likely to experience success if we develop first and then select.* By creating developmental environments where we attempt to create high learning conditions for all employees, as Bennis and Nanus (1985) suggest, we can select managers on the basis of actual performance rather than potential. In this way, more people have an opportunity to be considered for key positions, and the majority are not turned off. And there will be no select group which is playing it safe. This strategy would develop the entire organization, not just individual candidates.

Robert Hayes (1985) advocates this focus on resources (which he calls "means") as a starting point in strategy, rather than ultimate objectives ("ends"). He argues that the excessively rational/logical planning approach of working from ends to ways to means has been out of touch with the "real world" of everyday management:

> My point is not to disparage the relevance of all logic to planning, but to suggest that there may be alternative logics worth exploring. One of them, in fact, is to turn the ends-ways-means paradigm on its head: means-ways-ends.

> How might such a logic work? First, it suggests that a company should begin by investing in the development of its capabilities along a broad front (means). It should train workers and managers in a variety of jobs; educate them about the general competitive situation and the actions of specific competitors; teach them how to identify problems, how to develop solutions for them, and how to persuade others to follow their recommendations. It should acquire and experiment with new technologies and techniques so that workers and managers gain experience with them and come to understand their capabilities and constraints. It should focus R&D activity on fewer lines but spread it more widely throughout the organization. Managers should have cross-functional assignments so that they develop a broad understanding of the company's markets, technologies, and factories.

> Second, as these capabilities develop and as technological and market opportunities appear, the company should encourage managers well down in the organization to exploit matches wherever they occur (ways). Top management's job, then, is to facilitate this kind of entrepreneurial activity, provide it with resources from other parts of the company, and, where feasible, encourage cooperative activities. In short, the logic here is: 'Do not develop plans and then seek capabilities; instead build capabilities and then encourage the development of plans for exploiting them. Do not try to develop optimal strategies on the assumption of a static environment; instead, seek continuous improvement in a dynamic environment.' (Hayes, 1985, p. 116).

7. Create Diversity and Surprise throughout the Career

One of the important ways to create this diversity and learning in the internal environment is to adopt a human resource movement policy of lateral movement (Hall, 1984). Individuals would not be allowed to spend their entire careers in one functional area or specialty. By moving people every five years (or so) into areas demanding a different set of skills, learning would be demanded by the job. Familiar, scripted methods of solving problems would not always work in these new areas, so the individual would learn adaptive skills in the natural process of making the transition into each new area. These are critical skills for successful executives (McCall and Lombardo, in press).

These job changes would also force the person to examine issues of personal identity, since it would not be so easy to identify with a professional speciality. Or if the organization kept open the option of pursing a specialist career only as a conscious personal choice (and not by default, as is often now the case), this would encourage serious self-assessment and personal learning as part of that choice process.

8. Use a Wider Variety of Environmental Learning Methods for Executives

Implicit in what we have been saying about strengthening the developmental action component of the review process is the idea that there is a much wider range of environmental learning methods available to executives than most executives or companies utilize. There is great unused potential in the *natural learning opportunities* provided in the everyday organizational environment: task forces, project teams, temporary assignments, internal consulting projects, mentoring (as either the mentor or protege), rotational or cross-functional assignment, etc. As we said earlier, classroom learning is generally overused, and the work environment can be tapped much more than it is to enhance executive learning (Thompson et al., 1985). But these environmental methods need to be linked clearly to specific learning objectives.

CONCLUSION

In conclusion, organizations will have to broaden their definitions of executive learning. Personal learning (attitudes and identity) will be at least as important as new task skills for performance and adaptability. By giving the individual executive more responsibility for his or her own learning and career, by stressing more behavioral learning, and by creating less selective, more developmental learning environments throughout the organization, the growth of both the individual and the organization can be enhanced.

Executive learning should be facilitated through *learning environments*, not just through discrete, time bounded experiences such as executive development programs. The firm should stress on-the-job development of large numbers of young managers, not just fast-trackers. There will then be a much larger pool to select from for future senior positions. The more the organization can create diversity and surprise throughout the executive's career, the more learning will be "built in" to the basic fabric of the organization.

This executive learning will have to be tied in more to an ongoing process of strategic succession planning to replace key executives, as opposed to one-shot staffing or replacement planning. To make succession planning strategic, it will be necessary to identify in a systematic way the most likely future objectives for the firm and the executive skills necessary to lead the firm to the attainment of these objectives. A strong role in this process should be played by a senior human resource professional with expertise in executive job analysis.

Linking executive succession and development more consciously to the business strategy is thus the "acid test" of the firm's strategic planning process. It is not unusual now to see organizations commit and redeploy major financial and physical assets (e.g., product decisions, acquisitions, divestitures, plant closings) on the basis of their strategic objectives. However, the ultimate step in strategic management is the commitment of executive human resources. When a newly-appointed division head or a CEO is a person whose skills and style are a clear fit with the stated strategic direction of the firm, this represents final proof, internally and externally, that the strategy is for real. Succession actions speak far louder than strategic words.

Douglas T. (Tim) Hall is a Professor of Organizational Behavior in the School of Management at Boston University. He received his B.S. degree from the School of Engineering at Yale University and his M.S. and Ph.D. degrees from the Sloan School of Management at M.I.T. He has held faculty positions at Yale, York, Michigan State, and Northwestern Universities. At Northwestern he held the Earl Dean Howard Chair in Organizational Behavior and served as department chairman. He is the author of Careers in Organizations *and co-author of* Organizational Climates and Careers, The Two-Career Couple, Experiences in Management and Organizational Behavior, *and* Human Resource Management: Strategy, Design, and Implementation. *He is a recipient of the American Psychological Association's James McKeen Cattell Award for research design. He is a Fellow of the American Psychological Association and of the Academy of Management, where he served on the Board of Governors. He has served on the editorial boards of five scholarly journals. His research and consulting activities have dealt with career development, women's careers, career burnout, and executive succession. He has served as a consultant to organizations such as Sears, AT&T, American Hospital Supply, General Electric, Borg-Warner, Price Waterhouse, Ford Motor Company, Eli Lilly, and the World Bank.*

REFERENCES

Argyris, C. Human relations in a bank, *Harvard Business Review*, 1954, **32**, 63–72.

Argyris, C. *Personality and organization.* NY: Harper, 1957.

Argyris, C. *Reasoning, learning, and action.* San Francisco: Jossey-Bass, 1982.

Argyris, C., and Schön, D. *Theory in practice: Increasing professional effectiveness.* San Francisco: Jossey-Bass, 1974.

Argyris, C. "Bridging economics and psychology: The case of economic theory of the firm." Unpublished paper, Harvard University, 1986.

Argyris, C. *Strategy, change, and defensive routines.* Boston: Pitman, 1985.

Bartunek, J. M., and Louis, M. R. "Information processing activities associated with organizational newcomers' complex thinking." Working Paper No 85-12, Center for Applied Social Science, Boston University, November 1985.

Beck, R. "Strategic change at Bank of America." Symposium presentation, Annual Meeting of the Academy of Management, San Diego, 1985.

Bennis, W., and Nanus, B. *Leaders: The strategies for taking charge.* New York: Harper & Row, 1985.

Bolt, J. R. Tailor executive development to strategy, *Harvard Business Review*, November–December, 1985, **63**, 168–176.

Campbell, R. J., and Moses, J. C. Careers from an organizational perspective. In D. T. Hall and Associates, *Career development in organizations.* San Francisco: Jossey-Bass, 1986.

Casey, D., and Pearce, D. (Eds.). *More than management development: Action learning at GEC.* New York: AMACOM, 1977.

Executive grooming is a formal management process at some companies. *Wall Street Journal*, July 9, 1985, p. 1.

Friedman, S. D. *Succession systems and organizational performance in large corporations.* Unpublished doctoral dissertation, University of Michigan, 1984. (Revised version published as monograph: *Leadership succession systems and corporate performance.* New York: Center for Career Research and Human Resource Management, Columbia University, 1985.)

Friedman, S. D. Succession systems in large corporations: Characteristics and correlates of performance. *Human Resource Management*, 1986, 25, 191–213.

Gupta, A. K. Matching managers to strategies: Point and counterpoint. *Human Resource Management*, Summer 1986, **25**, in press.

Hall, D. T. Breaking career routines: Midcareer choice and identity development. In D. T. Hall and Associates, *Career development in organizations.* San Francisco: Jossey-Bass, 1986, in press.

Hall, D. T. Human resource development and organizational effectiveness. In C. Fombrun, N. Tichy, and M. A. Devanna, *Strategic human resource management.* New York: John Wiley & Sons, 1984, 159–181.

Hall, D. T. Project work as an antidote to career plateauing in a declining engineering organization, *Human Resource Management*, 1985, **24**, 271–292.

Hall, D. T. *Careers in organizations.* Glenview, IL: Scott, Foresman, 1976.

Hayes, R. H. Strategic planning—Forward or reverse? *Harvard Business Review*, November–December 1985, **63**, 111–119.

Iacocca, L. *Iacocca: An autobiography.* New York: Bantam Books, 1984.

Kanter, R. M. *Men and women of the corporation.* New York: Basic Books, 1977.

Kaplan, R. "Executive Self-development." Presentation at Career Division Workshop, Annual Meeting of the Academy of Management, San Diego, 1985.

Kaplan, R. E., Drath, W. H., and Kofodimos. *High hurdles: The challenge of executive self-development.* Greensboro, NC: Center for Creative Leadership, Technical Report No. 25, April 1985.

Katz, R. L., Skills of an effective administrator, *Harvard Business Review*, September–October, 1974, **52**, 90–102.

Kegan, R. *The evolving self: Problem and process in human development.* Cambridge, MA: Harvard University Press, 1982.

Korman, A. K., and Korman, R. W. *Career success and personal failure.* Englewood Cliffs, NJ: Prentice-Hall, 1980.

Levinson, D. J., and Associates. *Seasons of a man's life.* New York: Knopf, 1978.

Louis, M. R. "Surprise and sense making: What newcomers experience in entering unfamiliar organizational settings," *Administrative Science Quarterly*, 1980, **25**, 228–251.

Mahler, W. "Effective executive succession planning." Presentation at *Business Week's*, Third Human Resource Conference, May 19–21, 1982, New York Hilton, New York City.

McCall, M. W., Jr., and Lombardo, M. M. "What makes a top executive?" *Psychology Today*, April 1983, 82–86.

McCall, M. W., Jr., Lombardo, M. W., and Morrison, A. M. *The lessons of experience.* New York: Harper & Row, in press.

Renier, J. Presentation at Annual Meeting of Academy of Management, San Diego, 1985.

Saklad, D. Manpower planning and career development at Citicorp. In L. Dyer (Ed.), *Careers in organizations.* Ithaca, NY: New York State School of Industrial and Labor Relations, Cornell University, 1976, 31–35.

Schneider, B., and Schmitt, N. *Staffing organizations*, Second Edition. Glenview, IL: Scott, Foresman, 1986.

Thompson, P. H., Kirkham, K. L., and Dixon, J. Warning: The fast track may be hazardous to organizational health. *Organizational Dynamics*, Spring 1985, **13** (4), 21–33.

Concerns of the CEO*

Edward H. Bowman

Interviews with 26 CEOs across a wide variety of industries reveals their concerns as well as agenda and behavior. The issues discussed have been placed against four intellectual frameworks to get a better picture of CEO concerns. These executives frequently ponder institutional and corporate strategy but very seldom business strategy and competitive markets. The plurality of the concerns deal with issues of management development and human resource management. Where the question is one of changing or redirecting the strategy of the firm, it is often put in the context of looking inside the firm at top managers and organization culture.

INTRODUCTION

For anyone trying to understand the behavior of corporate chief executive officers (CEOs) it would seem useful to explore their concerns. While behavior, to be sure, does not flow directly from concerns, one could argue there is a loosely coupled chain from concerns, to agenda, to behavior. John Kotter (1982), in his study of a dozen general managers, summarizes their activities as setting the agenda, and establishing the network—and then ultimately, using the network to address the agenda. The reader is left with the importance of setting the agenda. However, there may be a substantial difference between passive concerns and a proactive agenda.

Even the gap between agenda and behavior (much less concerns) is nicely illustrated by Igor Ansoff in his early book, *Corporate Strategy* (1965), with his *New Yorker* quote "from the diary of a lady,"

Long-Range Goals:

1) Health—more leisure
2) Money
3) Write book (play?)—fame ////??
4) Visit India

* I would like to thank all of the CEOs interviewed and four colleagues at The Wharton School for critical comments on this paper, David Bussard, Stewart Friedman, Bruce Kogut, and Declan Murphy; and the Reginald Jones Center for its support.

Immediate:

Pick up pattern at Hilda's.
Change faucets—call plumber (who?)
Try yogurt??

For a starting point in understanding CEOs, I thought it would be useful to talk with them about their concerns. The Reginald Jones Center at Penn's Wharton School has as its research and education charter, "the concerns of the CEO." I have now interviewed 26 such people. They have come from a wide variety of companies and industries. Most of the companies are large, publicly owned and traded, and would be recognized by the typical business reader, either manager or academic. I have assured these people of confidentiality and so shall list neither the CEO nor the company name. Four of the people were recently retired (but active) CEOs. Two were European cases (but seemed much like Americans). Several of the 26 were either chairmen or presidents but not officially the CEO, though seemed willing and able to speak as though they were.

Banks, conglomerates, telecommunications, chemical, industrial equipment, automotive supply, pharmaceutical, electrical, petroleum, financial intermediary, public accounting, consulting, food processing, paper, and pipeline companies were all included in what is sometimes felicitously called a convenience sample. The smallest would be close to $100 million sales and the largest about $10 billion (two orders of magnitude difference), with the median and half the companies between $500 million and $1 billion. One thing which is surprising is that to the best of my recollection only one CEO turned down my request for the interview.

The interviews typically lasted from one to two hours. Several had more than the two of us present for the interview. The interview was loosely structured with my initially getting started with "what are your concerns?" This question triggered, very often, a long discourse with only the most minor prodding on my part, with a purpose not to bias the response. To return to the three-fold set at the start, the CEOs sometimes described what I will call concerns, sometimes agenda and sometimes behavior. One CEO initially said "I don't have any concerns, but I'll tell you what I do." He then proceeded to lay out for me an agenda of about eight items which he had recently discussed with the board, all in the context that they had a first class COO (chief operating officer) and that the CEO chose not to get involved any longer in operations.

Many of the interviews varied widely across a broad set of issues which permit no simple classification or description. I am reminded of a comment that Professor Mike Piori, an MIT labor economist, made in the *Administrative Science Quarterly* (1979). He had also started an interviewing process, and discovered that most people have a story they want to tell—regardless of the nominal questions which get them started.

> At first, I developed an elaborate list of questions for this 'preliminary' part of the interview, but I quickly found that the questions had very little to do with the success or failure of the interview. As I learned much later in a write-up of one of the Hawthorne experiments, most people had a story to tell. The interviewees used my questions as an excuse for telling 'their' stories.

Even so, I felt that along with these stories I was able to get a response to my basic questions about concerns.

Why should we be curious about the concerns (and agenda and behavior) of the CEO? The first reason is the obvious one that they wield a lot of power, and influence the performance of their corporations. I believe this, notwithstanding two different and important schools of thought, the one internally oriented of bureaucratic capture and the other externally oriented of overwhelming forces. The first follows the president-in-sneakers picture by Graham Allison in *Essence of Decision* (1971) (rather than the president-in-boots) running around trying to convince his associates of appropriate action. The second comes from the social (population) ecologists' view as fully layed out in Pfeffer and Salancik, *The External Control of Organizations* (1978), and illustrated by the quote from *The Strategic Management Journal* (1983) from Dirsmith and Covaleski, "In summary, we would prescribe that strategists give up the illusion of being in control of the process by which policies are developed. Organizational survival fundamentally involves fitting in with life and as such, must involve carrying on a robust dialogue with members of the environment." Even with some constraints on the CEO which certainly exist, I believe the chief executive makes a difference. On the basic philosophical question of free will vs. determinism, I'll stake out a place somewhere at midpoint. If one chooses the polar point of determinism, why ever fire top managers?

Any primary research method, including interviewing, faces the task of separating the real from the ideal. Jerome Bruner, in his interesting autobiographical book, *In Search of Mind* (1984) refers several times to the work of Jean Piaget, the Geneva child psychologist who explores as the major task of the child the continuing reconciliation of the mind (inner) and the world as experienced (outer). Bruner, looking at his own research, raises the somewhat rhetorical question about observation, "What does it tell us about the world, and what does it tell us about the mind?" Our study of CEOs faces these same issues, with the tentative conclusion that sometimes the listener is observing the mind, and sometimes the world. In fact, some CEOs seem to exemplify one side of this polarity or the other. This polarity between the idealist and realist seems also to characterize Presidents of the United States—between the Realpolitik pragmatism of Nixon–Kissinger and the moral (liberal) position of Carter or the moral (conservative) position of Reagan [see Schlesinger (1985)].

Arguing that the CEO has a major effect on the organization, I would especially mention the appropriate interest of the top staff people in the large American corporation, in his concerns. To be sure, the top general managers may emulate, substitute for, and perhaps replace the CEO; the top staff people are there to inform, help, and facilitate CEO activities. People/functions here would include Human Resources, Strategic Planning, R&D, General Counsel, and Finance. These people can be more effective in their special tasks if they understand *their* CEO's concerns somewhat better.

CONCERNS

There are many theoretical constructs or concepts into which one can fit the concerns that CEOs address. Several of these theoretical constructs will be used here shortly to help frame these concerns in different ways. First, however, it may be useful to simply list the 40 concerns that the 26 CEOs talked about. This list, of course, has required some interpretation, separation, aggregation, coding, and labeling on my part. They are listed in descending order of times mentioned as noted:

1.	Management development	(16)	21.	CEO job termination	(2)
2.	Strategy change or		22.	Peer approval	(2)
	recalibration	(10)	23.	Alliances (outside)	(2)
3.	Personnel problems/motivation	(10)	24.	Rate of change	
4.	Communications (inside)	(7)		(Society)	(2)
5.	Technology and R&D	(7)	25.	Divestments	(2)
6.	International		26.	Competition	(2)
	internationalization	(7)	27.	Customers	(2)
7.	Take-over (unfriendly)	(6)	28.	Energy problems	(1)
8.	Board matters	(6)	29.	Ethical issues	(1)
9.	Earnings	(6)	30.	Externalities	(1)
10.	Strategic planning system	(6)	31.	Academia	(1)
11.	Government	(5)	32.	Shareholder value	(1)
12.	Organization ("structure")	(5)	33.	Consultants	(1)
13.	Management succession	(4)	34.	Coordination	(1)
14.	Representation (external)	(3)	35.	Manufacturing	(1)
15.	Allocation of resources	(3)	36.	Quality	(1)
16.	Acquisitions	(3)	37.	Data processing	
17.	Culture	(3)		systems	(1)
18.	Diversification	(3)	38.	Buildings	(1)
19.	Evaluation	(3)	39.	Compensation systems	(1)
20.	Hazardous materials	(2)	40.	Liability insurance	(1)

On reading the many pages of notes taken from these interviews, it becomes obvious that all CEOs don't talk about the same concerns. Taking the 142 concern-counts and dividing by 26 people yields an average of 5 to 6 concerns noted, and there is really only a small variance around this number (it's close to the "the magic number 7" that psychologists talk about for memory recall). Though the set of concerns mentioned differed between CEOs by person, the interviews, in retrospect, didn't seem that different in style.

Before these concerns are described individually and in more detail, it is useful to look at them on a large scale. Several things stand out. The issues of management development clearly take first place as an area of concern, especially when combined with personnel problems which cover the total organization. They are the only concern mentioned by over half the people. The CEOs appear people oriented, especially with the people they know well. Second place goes to the strategic positioning of the whole company (as distinct from the divisions or strategic business unit). Here the issue is "content" and not "process," as strategic planning systems are further down the list.

At the other end of the spectrum, and as interesting, is what is discussed very little. What some commentators consider the backbone of the business, marketing and operations (or manufacturing), is little noted. Issues of business strategy and competitive advantage are almost nonexistent. Considering the current interest in and writing about such issues, one might anticipate more mention of them. Until one gets about a third of the way down the list in number count, the CEO orientation is commonly inside the company rather than outside or on the border. Finally, issues of social impact and social concern are largely missing. It is well to mention that these interviews were not directed with questions such as, "Are you concerned about . . . ?"

The ordered list of CEO concerns is interesting, but it may be more useful to reflect them against some of the constructs we presently entertain about management and managers. There are a number of conceptual or theoretical ways to frame the 40 CEO concerns (which have been listed by count). Four rather different frameworks will be used here for explication: (1) stages of planning, (2) levels of strategy, (3) roles of the general manager—CEO, and (4) arenas of economic decision making activity—politics, markets, and hierarchies.

1. Stages of Planning

Gluck et al. (1980) and his associates at McKinsey, Kaufman, and Walleck, have an interesting article "Strategic Management for Competitive Advantage" in the *Harvard Business Review*, which lays out the historical stages of planning for most companies—in sequence: 1) financial planning (budgeting), 2) long range planning, 3) strategic planning, and 4) strategic management. These historical stages are offered as stages in sophistication and usefulness as well. Not too many years ago, budgeting was the essence of planning for most companies. Long range planning both extended the time period as well as introduced all functions of the business to the planning process on a coordinated basis. Strategic planning introduced a systematic consideration of the external setting and environment of the firm—largely but not entirely economic and technological. With this process often came an explicit reconsideration of the organization structure of the company, introducing a decentralized structure with component labels such as strategic business units (SBUs) and portfolio management. Strategic management as a considered process placed new emphasis on the issues of implementation of the chosen strategies with the required attention to structure, people, information systems, measures, and rewards. As in any intellectual construct applied to the real world there tends to be overlap in both the ideal and the real among categories. There is at least some possibility that the nature of CEO concerns is in part influenced by changes in the nature of the planning systems employed. It may be a stretch of our results from the interview notes, but it appears that most concerns are at the advanced end, "strategic management." Comments from our interviews can be offset against each of these stages of planning.

Financial planning and budgets on a short term basis as a concern is illustrated by several CEOs, both involved in turnaround situations. One banker brought in to stem losses was faced with many bad loans and an unwieldy and fat organization. He paid attention first to these problems and at the same time started to address what he thought might be the underlying problem—extremely poor and fragmented computer/management information systems. The CEO of a small pharmaceutical manufacturer also had to move the organization from loss to profit and gave himself a year to do it. It was done in part by displacing executives. Now he is concerned with developing the remaining executives (this separation of those that go and those that stay is good Machiavelli, *The Prince*), and secondly, finding a strategic niche that will permit a competitive advantage in a growing market.

Long range planning (see Gluck, 1980) is a concern for a coordinated provision for all parts of the business over perhaps a five year period. This can be illustrated by several CEOs in their treatment of technology. One had felt that this was an area that had been slighted by his firm. Recently he had taken on supervision of this as one of his major tasks and had appointed an executive to the new job of Vice President, Technology. For the first time, technology is now being formally included in the long range plans made each year for the company. A second CEO now explicitly goes outside of this country to find the latest in technology for future needs. He claims he finds these answers in Japan and Belgium.

Strategic planning (a la Gluck, 1980; and others) involves a systematic look *outside* of the company at competitors, customers, etc. Two CEOs can illustrate this stage in planning. They both strongly reflect exposure to the consulting community, especially the Boston Consulting Group

(BCG). One argues strongly for the efficiency of SBUs (strategic business units) which can be calibrated to their own market place, as well as for the use of the PIMS (profit impact of market strategy) data base for comparative purposes, ". . . can't we squeeze more overhead out of operations?" A second CEO who explicitly discusses his competition in his various businesses and their market share is somewhat bemused by the implications of the BCG analysis. He drew some graphics on the blackboard and had data on what he claimed represented all American industry, and argued that two thirds of all America's SBUs are in the low growth low market share category referred to as dogs. Such divisions are one of his own concerns.

Strategic management, the fourth stage of Gluck's (1980) quartet, involves concern for successfully implementing the strategies developed. This includes choice and development of people, organization arrangements, information systems, and rewards. In a sense, much of what I heard spoke to these issues. These will be explored subsequently, especially the concerns of human resource management. Two concerns as problems in this domain will be offered here as illustrations. They were often problems not quite yet "found." When CEOs talked of management development, they were often not sure of the scope (or method) of the issue. One chairman of a chemical company who emphasized this issue allowed that they felt the best way to develop middle managers was to send them abroad to an international subsidiary in a general management position for five to seven years. He still felt that his top managers, many of whom were engineers, didn't have sufficient intellectual breadth. Another CEO, of a chemical company, was dismayed that they had hired a consultant that "came in and found many improvements that saved tens of millions of dollars" and "these improvements were staring the middle managers in the face and they didn't (and should have) recognize them."

While there are similarities between them, each stage of planning focuses on different issues. Each such set of focus issues can be illustrated from the CEO interview comments. Other ways of separating focus issues will now be described.

2. Levels of Strategy

A different set of intellectual constructs than stages in the planning process, are levels of strategy. Many authors talk about these with the common distinction between "corporate strategy" and "business strategy." To these can be added "functional strategy" and "enterprise strategy." Igor Ansoff, an early writer about *Corporate Strategy* (1965), supplied the title for "enterprise strategy" and I use this here (see Ansoff's chapter in Schendel and Hofer, editors, 1979, *Strategic Management: A New View of Business Policy and Planning*). Starting, then, with the most general and going to the most specific, the four levels of strategy (at least that one finds in the literature) are: A) enterprise strategy, B) corporate strategy, C) business strategy, and D) functional strategy.

Alfred Chandler has written the exemplar history book in strategy, *Strategy and Structure: Chapters in the History of the Industrial Enterprise* (1962) and shows among other things that business in this country historically grew through the strategy stages in the ascending order starting with functional strategy (a manufacturer only with others distributing for him), then to business strategy (all the functions of manufacturing, marketing, finance, technology development, personnel in one company), then to corporate strategy (with several or many different businesses requiring divisionalized decentralized structure). When his book was written in 1962, he included very little of what might be called enterprise strategy (the fitting of the corporation comfortably into the body-politic). Apparently, from La Belle Epoque to the Second World War there was not enough question of legitimacy according to Chandler to worry about enterprise strategy. Now that seems no longer true.

Enterprise strategy deals with the issues of fitting the corporation into its complete external environment including legal, political, and social. It involves the interactions with a wide variety of groups, some more powerful than others—now apparently carrying the label of stakeholders.

Corporate strategy involves the issues of managing the various interactions and reinforcements among the portfolio of (somewhat) separate businesses. These issues include resource allocation, coordination and economies of scope, synergy, transfer prices, effectiveness measurement, and capital flows. Also perhaps included are technology, international, acquisitions, and divestment.

Business strategy treats a particular business and the key actors in its product market—customers, competitors, suppliers, potential entrants, and substitutes (see Porter, 1980). Also considered are growth direction, generic strategy, competitive advantage, and make or buy decisions.

Functional strategy addresses the major issues in various functions such as marketing, manufacturing, finance and accounting, and human resources. Policy would often be a term employed in this context.

Taking these four levels of strategy reveals a remarkable picture of CEO concerns. With the one exception of treating all "Human Resource" issues separately from the other functions and categorizing all 142 concern-counts yields:

A) Enterprise Strategy	23
B) Corporate Strategy	56
C) Business Strategy	4
D) 1. Functional Strategy	13
2. Human Resources	45

In large companies, as many of these were, it is perhaps not surprising, even if true, that the CEOs do not dwell on business strategy. (Our count here was the two customer mentions and the two competitor mentions). Corporate strategy, on the contrary (and using our schema), was the most evident as source(s) of concern.

Even the relatively high count of enterprise strategy includes here concern for unfriendly takeovers, which some would classify as an issue of corporate strategy. (No formal strategic planning system we discussed with the CEOs included this issue in its format). Illustrations will be offered from our interviews for concerns at all of these four levels of strategy. Obviously space permits only a sample of such offerings, and their relative number counts have already been given individually in descending order, and collectively for the four levels.

The enterprise strategy level of concerns, by our classification scheme, tells of the issues and problems of comfortably fitting the firm into the environment—legal, political, social. Several examples of concerns across a wide spectrum will be offered. Several CEOs mentioned the time demanded to "represent" their firm at various community gatherings. *Pro bono publico* was to some extent the demand, almost a personal demand on his time—"too much." I asked why not send the Vice President of Public Affairs (or similar title), and the response was "they want number one." This demand is at the level of the city, the state, and the nation. Charitable, cultural, and industry professional were the occasions. Though the CEOs felt almost affronted by some of these demands, they attempted to respond supportively. They felt they couldn't do otherwise, for reasons of both their own and the firm's reputation.

Mentioned in other contexts later is the need to testify at congressional hearings in Washington about legislation and regulation issues. The concern of the chemical industry, broadly defined, with hazardous materials and wastes, Superfund, and subsequent/projected legislation is apparent. It was mentioned several times. What was also mentioned on more than one occasion is that these issues are not treated by the strategic planning processes and systems of the firm. Some CEOs take for granted and some bemoan the fact that what are here called enterprise strategy issues and concerns, including hostile takeovers, are not treated as part of the formal strategic planning process of the firm.

The Board of Directors was mentioned as a concern in a number of ways and by a number of CEOs. One mentioned keeping the board appropriately informed as an important concern of his. Another discussed the appropriate role of the Audit Committee and the interaction between top managers, accountants, and the public CPA firm. Finally, a retired/"consultant" CEO mentioned the concern of being on good terms, "sympathetic working arrangements," with individual board members. (The frankness of CEO discussion during the second or third hour of the interview often impressed me.)

The level of corporate strategy as treated here and as defined in most strategy textbooks encompassed the plurality of concerns of the CEOs interviewed. Where the CEO spoke of corporate strategy explicitly, he often talked of rearranging the portfolio of businesses to be pursued. Most of the firms visited had something analogous to an SBU structure. Many had been engaged in dismantling some of the SBUs. Some talked about adding new areas through an active acquisition program, though apparently it was usually the ad hoc prospect which surfaced.

Several interviewed CEOs mentioned international sourcing along the value-added chain as an area of concern. One of the CEOs felt chagrined as an American employer that he needed now to consider such possibilities. International competition from government-owned entities, which marched to different drummers, such as full employment rather than profit, were mentioned by several CEOs. Some CEOs mentioned concerns about joint ventures, and one even commissioned a study ". . . to describe and explain the various kinds of alliances which might have been used in the past such as the Hanseatic League. In ten years who knows who the partner might be of the goods manufacturer on the next shelf?"

As previously mentioned, the CEOs interviewed expressed almost no concern(s) about what is here classified as "business strategy." Borrowing from Michael Porter's (1980) ideas about competitive advantage and competitive actors such as customers, suppliers, potential entrants, substitutes, and direct competitors and strategic groups produced almost no mention. One has to assume that CEOs by and large feel these issues are in other capable hands in the firm and no sleep is lost here. A minor miscoding on the author's part may account for a small discrepancy, but not this large one. Nor is this explained by unusual profitability of the 26 firms contacted. At least a quarter of them were below nominal standards of profitability.

At the level of functional strategy as pictured here, and with the strong exception of human resource management, there was little mention of concern. Technology and R&D was also somewhat of an exception and here the exceptions end. Concerns were expressed by several CEOs as to their own understanding of the changing technology problems of the firm and the efficiency of the funds spent for R&D in the firm.

The major set of concerns placed here at the level of functional strategy is the area of human resource management. As counted, these were a third of the grand total. Included are management development, succession, motivation, compensation, evaluation, organization structure, and job definition, termination, and internal communication. All of these issues were *explicitly* mentioned as concerns. An implication of these comments is not only their importance but some dissatisfaction with the way these are currently addressed within the firm.

Management development concerns covered a broad spectrum of ideas. One CEO said, "Once a year the board goes through the top fifteen to twenty jobs for career development. The board gives us first class marks on this . . . The company is only as good as its management talent." Another said when they consolidated companies, they had to fire two of the three presidents. "They got beyond their span of control, their competence." Another listed first, "I'm concerned with the depth of management resources . . . we spend a lot of time on succession and work with the board on this." Another said, "The question is do we have the people in place to be truly industry leaders . . . Training in American business is a great area of tokenism." Another mentioned, "We had few whole managers and lots of partial managers. We relieved one division manager that had no street-smarts. He'd buy the Brooklyn Bridge three times." Another said, "We have to make sure that everybody understands that it (management development, and succession) is important. We put people's strength and needs down on paper. Rotation is my first answer to handle needs or weaknesses . . . I'm a little turned off by the MBO (management by objectives) type of thing."

In this context, but not listed above, are two CEO's concern with corporate culture (others also used the term). One CEO wanted to change the culture from a production culture to a marketing culture. He was a relatively new CEO who inherited a well established firm with an entrenched culture focused on manufacturing and manufacturing people. He is working hard to bring more emphasis to marketing, comparative product quality, competition, and the customer. He gives the impression that he has not yet made the transition to the extent that he wishes.

The second CEO wanted to maintain the culture and felt it slipping away. He had built a firm very successfully (not manufacturing), and as it grew he considered it becoming more "professionally managed" and more of a bureaucracy. In this discussion of human resources it is interesting that he lamented, "We even had to hire a Director of Human Resources." He much preferred the organic to the mechanistic, (Burns and Stalker, 1961) and he associated the move in styles with that hiring.

While the examples of specific concerns about Human Resource issues are too many to describe in detail here (but would not be unfamiliar to professionals in the field), the following list provides some insight:

- A lawsuit on age discrimination
- Executive training at universities
- Incentive compensation scheme for the top dozen people
- Lack of communication follow through 3 levels down
- Firing second tier executive(s)
- Job definition "between" the CEO and the COO
- New jobs to test several crown princes

- Performance evaluation ("very little validity")
- CEO job uncertain tenure
- Poor public schools to train future employees
- Send best middle managers abroad to develop
- Cut out layers of management (10 to 6)
- Peer acceptance
- Successor comfort with strategy moves
- Golden parachutes
- Openness (lack) of executive discussion
- Out of date manager
- Professionals hiring and keeping
- Bending the policies for exceptions
- Inadequate new number two man

Levels of strategy as just described are a useful way of looking at the problems of the firm. Many of these problems can also be mapped to the behavior of the individual executive. The unit of analysis now changes.

3. General Manager Roles

As a different cut from levels of strategy for us to explore CEO concerns, one of the most extensive empirical studies of general managers (essentially CEOs) was Henry Mintzberg's MIT Ph.D. thesis which became *The Nature of Managerial Work* (1973). He spent one full week observing each of five different general managers/CEOs. Sune Carlson's (1951) was a much earlier study done in Sweden (*Executive Behavior, A Study of the Work Load and the Working Methods of Managing Directors*), and John Kotter's (*The General Managers,* 1982) a later one. Among other constructs coming from this work, Mintzberg argues that these managers perform, simultaneously, ten identifiable and visible roles: a) *Interpersonal:* Figurehead, Leader, Liaison; b) *Informational:* Monitor, Disseminator, Spokesperson; c) *Decisional:* Entrepreneur, Disturbance handler, Resource allocator, and Negotiator.

Are these a useful way of explicating the concerns, agenda, and behaviors of CEOs? I believe they are and will attempt to illustrate each from my interviews:

1) *Figurehead* is illustrated by the concern that several executives expressed about all the time they had to devote to local charities and "cultural" affairs.
2) *Leader* can be illustrated by the chemical industry CEO, concerned about hazardous material, after Bhopal, communicating directly to plant managers several steps removed in the chain to immediately reduce hazardous inventories and straighten out the procedures and policies later.

3) *Liaison* fits with the concern which several CEOs have about their Boards of Directors seeing their role in part as a link to the Boards, as well as members of other boards which they described.

4) *Monitor* is seen as part of the concern with the strategic planning process, "I want to get close enough to the SBU managers to smell them."

5) *Disseminator* is part of a major concern with communications both outside but especially inside the organization feeling that the managers don't do it very well.

6) *Spokesman* ties in with the concern with government agencies and the legislative branch developing legislation for which testimony is required.

7) *Entrepreneur* is interesting as a concern because of its relative absence in mention, with an exception being the CEO who explicitly discussed it "looking for singles rather than home runs," with budget provision in the chairman's office to absorb especially promising innovation probes.

8) *Disturbance Handler* is illustrated by the rapid deployment of forces when the firm (several cases) was "invaded" by an unfriendly takeover threat, "It was all over in a week, and we didn't lose any executives."

9) *Resource Allocator* as mentioned elsewhere here is a concern for several CEOs to trade off between divisions while not losing the enthusiasm of the general managers.

10) *Negotiator* is interestingly absent in all 26 CEO interviews in the context of labor unions (not one concern mentioned), but is latent in many concerns, including Board relationships, acquisitions, succession, and others.

As explored by Professor Mintzberg, these identifiable roles may often be undertaken simultaneously. A CEO concern may fall across several of these roles. This is illustrated by the CEO of a large well known conglomerate when talking about buying and selling divisions, ". . . it's okay to sell divisions, but what are we going to do with the cash—buy other divisions at a premium—or buy back our stock like (another firm)?" He was touching on roles of leader, monitor, entrepreneur, resource allocator, and negotiator in our extended discussion of this one concern.

Because of the simultaneous roles as played against complex concerns, it is rather difficult to attempt an aggregate count as previously given for the levels of strategy. Reading through the interview notes would suggest that the leader role has the plurality of CEO concerns. This finding corresponds to the previous plurality of concerns with human resource issues, as well as the major point made in some of the more popular management literature such as Peters and Waterman's *In Search of Excellence* (1982).

4. Arenas of Economic Activity

Finally, we come to constructs which place CEO concerns in politics, markets, and hierarchies. Economic decisions and arrangements can be handled in several arenas including through political/governmental processes, in the various product and factor markets, and within the firm. Arguments can be offered about the appropriateness of each of these arenas depending on the issues and the circumstances, (and one's philosophy of political economy). To take the important topic of wages and salaries, one can find "decisions" made about aspects of these in all three places—politics, markets, and hierarchies. An executive concern may correspond to an issue in any of these arenas.

Charles Lindblom has written an interesting book, *Politics and Markets: The World's Political-Economic Systems* (1977), comparing the efficiencies of politics and markets for handling various problems which may be thought of as largely economic. He does a comparative analysis across a number of countries and political systems to make his case. If I understand his case, he would come down somewhat more on the side of politics than the typical American executive. Oliver Williamson has written a seminal book, *Markets and Hierarchies: A Study of the Economics of Internal Organization* (1975), comparing the efficient handling under various conditions of problems which might be thought of as economic. If I understand his arguments, he would come down on the side of hierarchies somewhat more than the typical economist. Joseph Bower has written an unusual book closing the circle—politics, markets, hierarchies (an otherwise straight line) called *The Two Faces of Management: An American Approach to Leadership in Business and Politics* (1983). Here he compares the style and substance of political managers and what he terms technocratic (read economic) managers. He makes the case for the appropriateness of the different styles and the need for each to understand the other (with some appropriate combinations of the two). We now have three positions on the circle; politics, markets, and hierarchies; and three books which sit between each set of two positions, Lindblom, Williamson, and Bower. Can we place CEO concerns against such schema?

I believe the concerns that at least three CEOs in the chemical and associated industries had about hazardous materials can clearly be placed in "politics." They acknowledge (and at the same time are somewhat apprehensive about) the role of government, national, state, and local to address these issues. The concerns and activities have been magnified following the Union Carbide tragedy at Bhopal, India. The Superfund legislation is now being considered for expansion. Hearings in both houses of Congress and committee industry surveys are taking place. "Right-to-Know" for community risk similar to worker risk is a current topic of discussion. The recent court conviction of three managers in Chicago for murder associated with a chemical process fatality has made the news. Surely these important issues, while they exist also in a market context (shall we move away from this product line?) and a hierarchies context (make the plant managers substantially reduce the dangerous inventories!), will be treated at the political level.

Several concerns of CEOs can be thought of appropriately at the level of financial markets. In addition to unfriendly takeovers, the concern for performance evaluation and the creation of stockholder value can be looked at through the mechanism of the stock market. A CEO of a major conglomerate, in mentioning performance evaluation as a concern, showed me a table which listed his company and its competitors on the ratio of market value to book value. He felt, and others feel, this is an important—perhaps ultimate—measure of corporate, and CEO, performance.

One concern mentioned by several CEOs was the allocation of resources between divisions. This can be thought of as an issue within the hierarchy. (Williamson argues that with the multidivision organization the well informed top management can do this better than the stock market). One president argues that in his firm this allocation is done even better *within* the divisions, a level down the hierarchy from the central office. Another CEO of a large "technology" company expresses as a major concern this allocation of resources between major divisions—by him—when he has convinced each group manager of the importance of his division, to "run it like he owned it" and then tell most of them they can't have all they ask for. When asked whether this issue was one of capital limitation, the answer was no, it was an issue of having the total corporate earnings grow each year.

One of the more interesting examples of CEO concerns which illustrates the framework of arenas of economic activity comes from a Scandinavian country. The CEO of an industrial equipment company described only three major concerns—and they map to the threefold arena framework—politics, markets, and hierarchies. The first concern he mentioned dealt with the problems of motivating people ". . . in the extreme welfare state." Absenteeism, separation, compensation, and alienation were major problems caused by the political system for him to deal with. The second issue had to do with their markets (and product lines). The several company businesses were in mature technologies and product/markets and he was concerned about diversification and acquisitions into which they had started to move. His third concern was R&D effectiveness. Did the organization (i.e., hierarchy) understand the appropriate places in which to place major funding to move ahead technologically?

Addressing the CEO concerns as judged against the arenas framework, they ranked by order count as hierarchies (87), markets (42), and politics (13). These order rankings may be largely explained by apparent immediacy and CEO sense of control. This is another way of illustrating that the concerns of the CEO focus largely inside the firm rather than outside.

SOME CONCLUSIONS

While I really want each reader to take away his or her own choice of ideas and conclusions from my research efforts, I shall offer some summary conclusions. Considering that many philosophers and psychologists have cautioned us against the various problems of understanding or describing what goes on in a person's mind (Gardner, 1985), I have chosen a rather straightforward approach of asking what are the concerns of the CEO. I argue that concerns start a loosely coupled chain, moving on to agenda, then on to behavior. *Language*, "representation," and the framing of issues, reflect these concerns, but in a rather profound and circular sense may also affect and influence these concerns, (Tversky and Kahneman, 1981; Bowman, 1982).

Rather than describe each CEO's response to our questions in interview sequence, the approach has been to organize the material against several received schema. This eclectic approach to the problems of epistemology has much to recommend it, (see Allison, 1971; and Bowman, 1974). The first, stages in the planning process reflect the historical development for most firms in dealing with formal planning systems. The stages focus on different issues and therefore it is possible to illustrate the stages with interview material from the CEOs. Strategic management is the stage where most of these concerns are noted.

The four levels of strategy were used in similar fashion, reflecting the locus of concerns. These levels are enterprise, corporate, business, and functional strategy. The distribution of concerns was an uneven one, revealing an especially low mention of concerns (and agenda) for business strategy, which could be described as how the firm will compete in a particular product-market, or sub-industry.

Corporate strategy, conversely, was the area of major concern, especially when issues such as acquisitions, mergers, and "takeovers" are included from enterprise strategy. How can a firm put together several or many businesses and through interactions, economies of scope, and management talent, capitalize on the advantages of the set? Conversely, what actions can the firm take to move away from maturing or failing product-market positions.

Using the idea of roles, and role theory, made possible the illustration of concerns across the broad set of roles played by the CEO, with perhaps no major focus discovered. The idea of arenas of economic activity—politics, markets, and hierarchies—did highlight the major concern with hierarchies, followed by markets, and then politics. If one is forced to declare a position, CEOs look more inside than outside the firm. However, issues spill across the three arenas, and salaries and wages were offered as an example. But a concern with unfriendly takeovers, which was discussed by six CEOs, even better illustrates the way an issue falls into all three arenas, politics, markets, and hierarchies, with the comments that the CEOs make about this concern.

Human resource management and more particularly, management development, stand out as the plurality of concerns for these 26 CEOs. They are concerned with the interplay between strategies and managers. Resolutions of concerns, both agenda and actions, often mean changing or restructuring groups of people.

As we have continued our interviews beyond the initial set, this result seems to be a consistent one. A second Scandinavian CEO recently interviewed and not itemized in the sample described had held the CEO title in three different Scandinavian firms in the last five or six years. He could readily describe his concerns in these three firms in different industries; a focused manufacturing company, a conglomerate, and a service organization. Upon reviewing my notes about each firm, the first thing which struck me was that his concerns (and agenda) were quite different among the three firms, and at least in this instance, a CEO does not "carry" a standard set of concerns across different situations, an observation that would please contingency theory enthusiasts. But secondly, toward the end of discussing each assignment, he went on to describe the people management aspect of the issues as something which he had to address, as a way to cope with the strategic issues. He did this unguided by me in all three instances.

What conclusions does one draw from all of this? A) I believe that for our work, levels of strategy as an idea has been the most useful scheme to understand the concerns of the CEO. B) I believe that the change in emphasis noticed in some of the business press, and consulting firms, from strategy formulation to strategy implementation, is important. C) I believe that the typical CEO looks inside rather than outside the firm to a greater extent than is commonly thought. D) Regardless of mental representation or language employed, the importance of people, human resources, or human capital to today's CEO is obvious.

WHO CARES?

In summary, the case is made here that it's important to understand CEO concerns in both a detailed sense and in a more generic sense. Three groups might especially change their response patterns to these CEO concerns, especially the heavy weighting of human resource management issues, but also other topics such as internationalization, government, technology, and unfriendly takeovers. The three particular response groups are a) the corporate planners with their annual plans formatting, b) the human resource managers with their development programs, and c) the business schools with their curricula.

If the academic professor or university center wishes to speak either to or about the firm, it seems short-sighted to miss the major actor. If the top staff vice presidents in the firm want to help and perhaps influence the CEO, it's useful to know the concerns found there—again of both a specific and generic nature. Where an open dialogue doesn't exist, perhaps a third party can get it started. Concerns usually lead to agenda which usually lead to behavior. Finally, I have found that CEOs are curious about the concerns of their fellow CEOs.

Edward H. Bowman is Reginald H. Jones Professor of Corporate Management at the Wharton School, University of Pennsylvania. He has been comptroller of Yale University and dean at Ohio State, as well as assistant to the president of Honeywell's computer company. He holds academic degrees from M.I.T., the University of Pennsylvania, Ohio State University, and Yale University.

REFERENCES

Allison, G. *Essence of Decision*, Boston: Little Brown and Company, 1971.

Ansoff, I. *Corporate Strategy*, NY: McGraw Hill, 1965.

Ansoff, I. "The Changing Shape of the Strategic Problem," in *Strategic Management: A New View of Business Policy and Planning*, Boston: Little Brown, 1979.

Bower, J. *The Two Faces of Management: An American Approach to Leadership in Business and Politics*, Boston: Houghton-Mifflin, 1983.

Bowman, E. H., Epistemology, Corporate Strategy, and Academe, *Sloan Management Review*, Winter 1974.

Bowman, E. H., Risk Seeking by Troubled Firms, *Sloan Management Review*, Summer 1982.

Bruner, J. *In Search of Mind*, NY: Harper and Row, 1984.

Burns, T., and Stalker, G. M. *The Management of Innovation*, London: Tavistock, 1961.

Carlson, S. *Executive Behavior: A Study of the Workload and the Working Methods of Managing Directors*, Stromberg, Stockholm, 1951.

Chandler, A. *Strategy and Structure: Chapters in the History of the Industrial Enterprise*, Cambridge: MIT Press, 1962.

Dirsmith, M. W. and Covaleski, M. A. "Strategy, External Communication and Environmental Context, *Strategic Management Journal*, April–June 1983.

Gardner, H. *The Mind's New Science: A History of the Cognitive Revolution*, NY: Basic Books, 1985.

Gluck, F. W., Kaufman, S. P., and Walleck, A. S. "Strategic Management for Competitive Advantage," *Harvard Business Review*, July–August 1980.

Kotter, J. *The General Managers*, NY: Free Press, 1982.

Lindblom, C. *Politics and Markets: The World's Political–Economic Systems*, Basic Books, Harper, 1977.

Mintzberg, H. *The Nature of Managerial Work*, NY: Harper and Row, 1973.

Peters, T. J., Waterman, R. H. Jr., *In Search of Excellence: Lessons from America's Best Run Companies*, NY: Harper and Row, 1982.

Pfeffer, J., and Salancik, G. R. *The External Control of Organizations*, NY: Harper and Row, 1978.

Piori, M. "Qualitative Research Techniques in Economics," *Administrative Science Quarterly*, December 1979.

Porter, M. *Competitive Strategy*, NY: Free Press, 1980.

Schlesinger, J. "The Eagle and the Bear: Ruminations on Forty Years of Super-power Relations," *Foreign Affairs*, Summer, 1985, **63**(5).

Tversky, A., and Kahneman, D. The Framing of Decisions and the Psychology of Choice, *Science*, January 30, 1981.

Williamson, O. *Markets and Hierarchies: A Study of the Economics of Internal Organization*, NY: Free Press, 1975.

The Dynamic Organizational Contexts of Executive Succession: Considerations and Challenges

———— Craig Lundberg ————

Given the increasing changefulness of organizational circumstances, the change and transition role of executives takes on increasing prominence. This essay describes the dynamic context related to the organizational life cycle, evolutionary and planned change, and cultural transformation. Executive roles that provide guidance for executive assessment and development, and especially for selection, are explicated.

INTRODUCTION

Thoughtful observers of organizational life have often described the careers, challenges, and fates of institutional leaders as well as speculated upon their organizational, institutional, and societal consequences. The business and general press chronicles newsworthy succession events almost daily and popular books detail the stories of prominent executives in all arenas—their rise and fall and surrounding circumstances seem to hold an intrinsic fascination for nearly everyone. Succession, in the guise of companion topics such as promotion, tenure, career, training and development, and a host of others is the grist of organizational rumor mills and the target of perseveration by members of all ages, occupations, and achievement. While long a topic of interest, in recent years organizational scholars and managers alike have been drawn more and more to the topic of executive succession.

Research into executive succession has recently both broadened and deepened its focus. Perhaps the major omission in the succession literature relates to the organizational context of succession. As the rate of change increases for society, markets, and industries, it is mirrored in organizations. To fully understand executive succession, therefore, we need to focus our attention on the dynamic organizational contexts to date relatively ignored: succession contexts related to organizational change and transformation within and between stages of the organizational life cycle. These areas are significant for two main reasons. First, many key environmental variables at the industry and economy level trigger, channel, and moderate an organization's movement through its life cycle; therefore, attention to the organizational life cycle may help us to understand how and why succession occurs. Secondly, the environments of all organizations are recognized as becoming more complex and variable, requiring ongoing organizational changes and sometimes even fundamental transformations. These in turn stretch and stress all members, especially executives, bringing basic patterns and practices into bolder relief, testing core values and assumptions. Organizational changes of all kinds, swift or slow, major or minor, are increasingly not only the common circumstances of executive succession, but imply competencies that successors require.

This admittedly exploratory article unfolds in three sections. In the first one, we review and map the dynamic contexts of interest here. Attention focuses on change contexts and processes that are planned or evolutionary and lead to major changes or even more fundamental transformations. The second section then turns to a discussion of the roles executives play in these processes and dynamic contexts and thereby suggests contingent criteria for successors. The third and final section of the essay presents some implications for executive selection and development as suggested by our attention to dynamic contexts.

The Dynamic Contexts of Succession

A current truism is that the reality of organizations is increasingly dynamic, that is, organizations are always experiencing and exhibiting change of some kind and magnitude (Bateson, 1979). Given the ubiquity and importance of change in organizations, executive succession needs to be better understood in such terms.

In this section we sketch four different dynamic contexts, differentiating them along two dimensions. In one dimension, changes may be viewed as natural/evolutionary or the consequence of intentional, that is, planned efforts. Here the difference is in the process of change— between changes that occur primarily reactively or opportunistically through everyday problem-solving activities, as opposed to those that are the result of proactive, focused change efforts. The second dimension is essentially the degree of impact that changes have on the organization's fundamental character. Here, elements of an organization may achieve a better fit with other elements (or the whole organization) on the one hand, or, on the other hand, there may be a shift in the organization's basic character, nature, and functioning. The former we term "organizational change." The latter is here labeled "organizational transformation," implying that an organization's culture or essential way of being undergoes alteration. With the two dimensions just noted, a two by two matrix which maps the four archetypical types of organiza-

| Nature of Change | Magnitude of Changes | |
Process	Change	Transformation
Evolutionary	"Efficiency and Effectiveness" I	"Strategic Drift" II
Planned	III "Adaptation"	IV "Cultural Alteration"

Figure 1. A Map of dynamic organizational contexts.

tional changes can be constructed as shown in Figure 1.* The four quadrants are labeled in terms of their primary outcomes.

The organizational changes that result from conventional, ongoing problem-solving practices (cell I) ostensibly enhance the organization's efficiency and/or effectiveness. Ongoing adjustments of this order, may, over time, accumulate incrementally (Quinn, 1980). When these micro-level changes are selectively reinforced by top management, the organization seemingly "drifts" into a different strategic posture, which can ultimately be seen as having transformative effects (cell II). Planned organizational change (cell III), while often necessitating many internal adjustments, is typically focused on achieving a better fit between the organization, its input and output domains, and its general environment, i.e., it is intended to achieve better adaptation. The social technologies of strategic planning and organizational development, among others, are well known adaptive devices. When adaptive responses are insufficient, that is, when the organization finds itself "surprised" (Schon, 1983) in the sense that its unquestioned values and assumptions about how the organization operates are violated, organizational cultural transformation (cell IV) may be triggered. Cultural transformation, of course, is relatively rare and only now is beginning to be understood (Schein, 1985; Frost et al., 1985; Kilmann, 1984; Kilman et al., 1985).

The dynamic contexts, characterized above as evolutionary and planned organizational changes, need not be further commented upon because they are both familiar and have well developed change technologies. Those contexts we have labeled as organizational transformation, however, require further explication. How does strategic drift occur? All organizations experience deviance, sometimes when required systems,

* The two dimensions, of course, really describe continua. We partition them as shown to more clearly reflect the differences which occur when the dimensions are combined.

structures, or processes intentionally or unintentionally are not adhered to and sometimes through innovations and experimentation. When such deviance occurs and appears functional, management may adopt or at least tolerate it. Those divergences that are reinforced by management's tolerance or blessing can, as they accumulate over time, result in macro-level changes, that is, the organization evolves (Weick, 1979). Note this "drift" is neither planned nor rationally conceived. The key for transformative evolution (i.e., strategic drift) is for these newer elements to be ultimately acknowledged and articulated by the organization's leaders as central to the character of the system (Kanter, 1985). This post hoc reframing (Watzlawick et al., 1974) of core cultural exemplars, beliefs, and values by the dominant coalition substitutes for and/or parallels organizational strategy (Weick, 1985) for both strategy and culture function to impose coherence, order, and meaning.

Planned organizational transformation, that is, managed culture alteration, requires the organization to "learn" (Argyris and Schon, 1978), in that its unquestioned, unconscious values and guiding beliefs (Davis, 1984) are made explicit and substituted with a new, supposedly more appropriate "vision." Lundberg (1985a) has outlined the internal and external conditions that enable organizational learning, the pressures which precipitate culture change (e.g., atypical performance demands, stakeholder pressure, organizational growth or downsizing, and real or perceived crises), and has cataloged five classes of trigger events: sudden environmental calamities, (e.g., natural disasters, sharp recession, major competitor innovations); opportunities (e.g., technological breakthroughs, newly available venture capital); internal and external revolutions; and managerial blunders (e.g., foolish expenditures, inappropriate tactics). Trigger events "surprise" in that they pose a "predicament"—unquestioned values and beliefs are recognized as being violated and inappropriate. Sometimes, the leaders enter into the non-ordinary activities of anticipating future conditions, creating a new image of their organization within that future, strategizing for the major transitioning implied, and action planning so that the multiple interventions necessitated impact the organization's deeper levels of meaning, as well as its surface or cosmetic ones.

Organizational change and transformation can and do occur at any time, given certain circumstances and stimuli. It seems useful, however, to note those predictable periods of relative stability and the periods of sharp transitions that organizations experience—a general process commonly referred to as movement through the organizational life cycle. Our state of knowledge about organizational life cycles is still rather modest. Various models each pose a different numbers of "stages," and they differ as to whether the sequence of stages is deterministic or not (e.g., Filley, 1962; Starbuck, 1971; Kimberly, 1979; Kimberly and Miles, 1980; Cameron and Whetten, 1981). Sequences tend to include a creation, growth, maturity, revival (sometimes), decline, and end set of

Movement in the Organizational Life Cycle

Magnitude of Changes	Within Stages	Between Stages
Organizational Change		
Organizational Transformation		

Figure 2.   The varieties of dynamic contexts.

stages (Miller and Friesen, 1980).* Schein (1985) argues, however, that from a cultural point of view, generational age, that is, the organization managed by the founder, succeeding family, and professional management in turn, is the important variable here. Here we will adopt Schein's (1985) three major developmental stages of (a) birth and early growth, (b) organizational midlife, and (c) organizational maturity and stagnation. The varieties of dynamic context are derived from a combination of the magnitudes of changes discussed previously with the idea that changes occur either within or between stages in the developmental sequence of the organizational life cycle, as shown in Figure 2.

With a map of the types of possible dynamic contexts, we can consider which of the cells of Figure 2 are likely to hold the most activity and which would seem to involve the most difficulty for managerial change agents. Clearly, organizational change within developmental stages is where most observed executive behavior lies—it is what management is mostly all about. This also is the area that most change-related knowledge and experience is about (i.e., the theory and practice of organizational development). There is probably considerable organizational change between stages too. Transformations are probably relatively rare events, though more likely to occur in the transition between stages of the organizational life cycle. Our understanding about transitioning and transformations at the present time is quite modest although some conceptualization and research has occurred (e.g., Kimberly and Quinn, 1984; Frost et al., 1985; Schein, 1985).

Thus far we have outlined the conception of dynamic contexts in which executive succession takes place and, no doubt, influences. While it was pointed out that change in general was either natural and evolving or planned, we also emphasized the differences between changes

---

* Movement through these developmental stages may range from swift to slow and vary, too. Stages may overlap somewhat, blurring transition or occasionally becoming sharply delineated.

which resulted in better adjustment and/or adaption and those which transformed the organization both strategically and culturally. In addition, we introduced a model of the organization life cycle so that changes within stages and during transition between stages could be more readily ascertained. Until this point we have not dealt with the processes of how changes and transformations actually occur, and it is to these processes that we now turn.

Change and Transformation Processes

It is axiomatic that all proactive changes begin with the organization's perception or experience of some environmental and/or internal threat, loss, or opportunity. These perceptions/experiences, however, are then interpreted as either "problems" or "predicaments"—the former leading to organizational change and the latter to organizational transformation.*

If the trigger event is a problem interpreted as necessitating organizational change, then some variant of a problem-solving or action-research process is followed, for example, the organization would become involved in: (a) mobilizing concern and inducing readiness for change, (b) fact finding and diagnosis, (c) searching for solutions or their invention, (d) intervention, and (e) assessment and the institutionalization of change. This process assumes several points: that it is initiated by persons with control of key resources; that the stress induced is relatively minor; that current objectives are sufficient; and that mutual adjustment of organizational elements to each other or the organization to its environment is the purpose. It is this last point, however, that is seldom adequately achieved and which over time permits strategic drift.

If the organization members' interpretation is that of a predicament, the transformational process previously termed cultural alteration tends to look somewhat different.† If there is sufficient concern within the dominant coalition to stimulate activity, then several things seem to occur more or less simultaneously. Resources are mobilized—resources of ideas, manpower, competencies, and so forth—beyond those needed for the ongoing operation of the organization. Activities are initiated which lead to the more or less systematic envisioning of the probable future environmental conditions of the organization. Leaders and their cohorts also go about surfacing the heretofore unconsciously held guid-

---

* Of course, the label "problem" is sometimes misleading since problem connotes solutionability. Some so-called problems are actually dilemmas or even paradoxes.

† This transformational process has been synthesized from the recent writings and presentations of E. Schein, T. Deal, W. Dyer Jr., C. Lundberg, J. Martin, C. Siehl, and P. Vaill.

ing beliefs, assumptions, and values of the organization. With resources mobilized, a future more or less conceived, and the deeper basis of identity and meaning of the organization acknowledged, a reframing or visioning of the organization's image, culture, or paradigm (Pettigrew, 1979; Pfeffer, 1981; Mohrman and Lawler, 1983) is defined by its leadership.

Once visioning or its product occurs, mourning for the old culture elements to be abandoned is initiated and guided. At the same time, power must be mobilized to translate the new vision into actuality (sometimes, of course, countervailing power structures are also mobilized). A strategy, that is, a general plan for transforming the present culture into the new one, is then devised as are the explicit action plans for intervening across all levels of meaning. This includes surface levels of meaning derived from artifacts, credos, and behavioral norms, to the levels of deeper meaning which reside in values, guiding beliefs, and assumptions. While all of this is going on, and thereafter, care must be exercised to involve organizational members, and importantly, the leadership must absorb their anxieties and provide ongoing reassurance. The sequence of multiple interventions at multiple levels of meaning then commences. When predicaments are absolved through strategic drift, much of the above takes place informally, even unconsciously, and the new state of affairs is articulated afterwards by the leadership (who usually take credit for the transformation). Regardless of whether the transformation is intended or evolves, continued espousal of the new culture is usually necessary (through stories, charters, slogans, symbols, etc.) in support of the pattern maintenance via altered structures, systems, management practices, and climate factors. This goal of persistence of performance over time leads to the existence of the new culture as established social fact (Goodman et al., 1980). Of course, as the transformation proceeds, problems can and do occur, signaling the need for the organizational change process to be activated. The processes of transformation and organizational change are summarized diagrammatically in Figure 3.

It should be emphasized that the processes as outlined above appear more spare, more linear, and more deterministic than the way they actually may be enacted. The sequence of activities may and often does overlap considerably, cycling back to the earlier steps may occur, and some of them may be accomplished informally or implicitly. The flow of activities outlined, however, does appear to be required for successful change or transformation to occur. Without somehow attending to each step in the sequence the processes become derailed, bogged down, and manifest only "pseudo" changes.

This somewhat lengthy review of dynamic contexts and processes has set the stage for probing their implications for executive succession. What executive behaviors seem to be called for by these dynamic contexts and their attendant processes? In the following section we respond

Figure 3.   The processes of organizational change and planned organizational transformation.

The Process of Organizational Change		The Process of Planned Organizational Transformation	
(1)	The perception of, or experience of internal or external loss, or opportunity	(I)	The perception of, or experience of internal or external loss, threat, or opportunity
(2)	Interpretation that there is a *problem*	(II)	Interpretation that there is a *predicament*
(3)	Mobilize concern and initiate readiness for change	(III)	Mobilization of concern among the dominant coalition
(4)	Fact finding and diagnosis	(IV)	a. Mobilization of transformative resources b. Envisualization of future environmental circumstances
(5)	Solution search or intervention	(V)	Surfacing of the organization's guiding beliefs, values, and assumptions
(6)	Intervention	(VI)	Design of transition strategy and tactics
(7)	Assessment and institutionalization of change	(VII)	a. Guidance of mourning for lost culture elements b. Mobilization of power
		(VIII)	a. Anxiety absorption and reassurance by leadership b. Intervention sequence activated
		(IX)	a. continued articulation of the new culture b. Initiation of pattern maintenance devices

to this question by an examination of the roles associated with change and transformation activities.

Executive Role Requirements in Dynamic Contexts

If some form of change is the predominant circumstance in which organizations increasingly find themselves, then they will find it advisable to attract and retain, as well as develop, executives who possess change and transformation competencies. The prior extended discussion of dynamic contexts and processes enables us to now consider the roles they require, each role suggesting distinctive selection criteria. We shall first note the roles and essential activities for each major stage of the organizational life cycle, and then in more detail, note those associated with the processes of organizational change and transformation.*

Executive Roles During the Organizational Life Cycle

Recall the developmental, generational age influenced organizational life cycle stages previously introduced: birth and early growth, organizational mid-life, and organizational maturity and stagnation. Organizations in the first of these stages find themselves struggling for an identity based on the development of a distinctive competence. Succession in this stage is colored, often strongly, by the person or ghost of the founder-culture creator. Founders and their successors need to articulate the organization's identity. They have to work continuously on its integration, relentlessly teaching other members that the organization is singular and unique. At the same time, founders and their successors must keep internal power struggles out and provide as much psychological safety for members as possible, given the normal turmoil that getting established as an organization entails. Successful successors often must resemble the founder in ways central to the emerging culture (members are prone to psychological projection here, of course). If succession is crisis initiated, however, then pronounced differences in style are recommended as long as the successor hews to those organizational core values that underscore its distinctiveness. Unless faced with calamity, the successor will be advised to endure the organization's culture and not attempt to alter it, for to do so risks member alienation.

An organization's agenda during its mid-life stage turns from establishing an identity and finding an environmental niche, to how to pursue growth, and with growth, how to prevent the organization from fragmenting. During this stage, executives and their successors must continue to reiterate the culture, usually indirectly through credos, slogans, and the like, and see to it that the new members acquire the beliefs and jargon that instill unity. With growth, subcultures will normally develop, and it is likely that parts of the organization will get into trouble. Executives will therefore be advised to champion ongoing assessment and insist on diagnosis as needed. They will also permit some internal power struggles, especially those that foster growth and/or redress any bias or imbalances left behind by the functions essential to the first stage. During the mid-life stage, cultural assessment is seldom attempted, the exceptions being when the organization experiences the trauma of merger or acquisition, major geographical expansion, or technological obsolescence.

---

* In what follows, we shall not discuss general management, technical, and business function competencies—all of which are equally vital for organizational health and survival.

As organizational maturity turns into stagnation (usually because of product obsolescence and market saturation), executives fill quite different roles. Creating psychological safety for members is the increasingly essential task, especially for those units that have become dysfunctional. An executive's symbolic roles take on increasing importance for the maintenance of morale and the support of a positive organizational image. It is also important that executives capture control of key resources and monitor their use carefully. With some chance of reprieve from stagnation, effective executives find ways to selectively encourage members who seek new products, markets, or any other innovation that promises relief from demise. Part of this process may also be executive role modelling, sponsorship of self examination, and selective renewal although members will be relatively immune toward such examination because their prior cognitive structures, norms, and games prohibit it (Nystrom and Starbuck, 1984).

Executives who attend to their organization's movement through the organizational life cycle, as has been noted, must be sensitive to several major issues: (a) when to actively work at building/defining the organization's culture and when to essentially leave it be with just recognizing and reinforcing it; (b) when to push for integration of organizational elements and sub-units and when to allow or even foster some inter-unit differentiation or struggle; and (c) when ongoing organizational change is sufficient and when transformation is called for. This last issue requires a sensitivity to the predicament potential of major events as well as to the natural approach of organizational life cycle stage endings. In general, executive sensitivity to these issues comes from an ongoing attention to a number of factors such as: his or her relationship with the organization's dominant coalition (Pfeffer, 1977), since having a power base is always essential; the preferences, constraints, and political pressures of the organization's stakeholders (Mason and Mitroff, 1981), since those must be factored into change endeavors; and, portions of the organization's history since expectations of leaders, the precedence value of part successes and failures, the crucial constraints in technology and the like, all provide guideposts to any change efforts undertaken.

Executive Change and Transformation Roles

Turning now to the outline of the processes of organizational change and planned transformation (cf. Figure 3), we inquire into the roles these processes require of executives and the criteria they imply for executive selection and development. Both processes begin in common with the perception or experience of loss, threat, or opportunity. Active scanning, surveillance, and ongoing intelligence activities of the past, the environment, and the organizational response are indicated.

The roles may be labeled "G2/U2" as shorthand for intelligence and surveillance. Both processes also have in common the interpretation of that which is perceived or experienced. To interpret appropriately necessitates considerable conceptual skill. Voicing the interpretation and being heard may in addition entail courage or boldness and the ability to risk. The role is that of "challenger" which continues on through the mobilization of concern (the initiation of readiness for the change process, and the mobilization of resources for transformation). Here, political skills and sensitivities come into play, and the role is characterized as one of being "godfather" or "lobbyist."

For organizational change the executive may also engage in goal clarification (or see that it is done) and assign one or more others the responsibility for going forward. Thereafter, he or she more or less actively "monitors" diagnosis, solution and search invention, and intervention—and plays "nudge" as needed. When change efforts have been implemented, assessment of their impact is advised though uncommon. Here the executive has to become a tough-minded "skeptic." If the change appears to be functional, its reinforcement and its degree of congruency with other elements means the executive initiates or plays "design" and "advocate" roles.

Organizational transformation, as noted, begins with roles of "G2/U2" and "challenger." It draws, early on, upon political sensitivities and skills. The transformation process begins to differ from organizational change at this point. Executives involved with transformation have to lead activities which produce useful scenarios of the organization's future environmental circumstances, and which produce the surfacing of the organization's present deep meanings. These are very difficult tasks, taxing of executive leadership. Executives must play some combination of "sponsor," "enthusiast," and "first violinist" as they guide the work which specifies the organization's future and current culture. The ability to synthesize information and to perceive themes, to in effect step outside of prevailing thoughtways, is pertinent, as is the ability to articulate discoveries. Someone, most often the executive, must provide the articulated eloquence that captures and inspires others. "Wordsmithing," therefore, is another role, one that carries forward throughout the transformation process.

The next transformation role is akin to an "orchestra conductor" (Galbraith, 1985), guiding the design of a process plan (Beckhard and Harris, 1977) for transition strategy and tactics. As a new image emerges and is communicated, members quite naturally begin to feel (even more strongly than earlier in the process) the anxiety associated with new uncertainties and the loss of familiar and comforting perspectives. The executive roles here are the critical ones of "eulogizer" for that which has been lost and "reassurer" that the future holds promise. From the decision that the organization faces a predicament, executives have to mobilize and channel the power to go forward. The role of power mobilizer is that of "sponsor," drawing other managers and their units into a constituency for transactioning. With the process well underway, the new focal themes, values, and associated practices require repeated articulation and the introduction of structures and systems which buttress them. Executives here must tenaciously enact the demanding roles of "pest" and "tire kicker"—seeing to it over time as the new culture's artifacts and norms become habitual and that members do not regress.*

The above activities and roles for change and transformation each implies criteria for executive selection. No one executive is likely to be able to perform all of these roles and probably should not be expected to do so. Selection of an executive, however, should strive to ensure that the whole complement of roles exists in the top management team and that the persons selected are competent in those critical roles common to all dynamic contexts and processes. These general, common roles take shape in six fundamental profiles: being a *cultural spokesman*, able to articulate, espouse, and interpret at several levels of meaning; being a *rascal* in the sense of calling for change or transformation and championing the new; being *power sensitive and politically adept* both during and after changing or transitioning; being able to *absorb anxiety* and provide reassurance; being able to call forth, enlist or do the *design* work that change and transformation require; and, being able to *persist* and keep others persisting until movement has once again become stability.

On Executive Selection and Development

The dynamic contexts, processes, activities, and roles elaborated in the prior discussion have implied differential criteria for executive behavior in a variety of circumstances. Now we turn to the processes of executive selection and development. In what follows we take as given that candidates for succession have general management competencies, sound conceptual and analytic abilities, and are familiar with the type of business and/or industry they are in.

The Succession Process

Executive succession may usefully be discussed in terms of three general questions: When does it occur? Is it anticipated or not? Who should

---

* Illustration and initial support for these executive roles and activities may be found in those relatively rich case descriptive accounts of managerial behavior in major organization change which are beginning to appear in the literature, e.g., Browne et al. (1982), Dyer (1984), Fombrun et al. (1984), Lundberg (1985a), Martin et al. (1985), Mirvis (1985), Siehl (1985), Tichy and Ulrich (1984), and Turnstall (1985).

be involved? The first question highlights the very subject of this essay—the dynamic contexts and associated processes. What is the stage of development of the organization, and is it nearing a point of transition to the next stage? Within the birth and early growth stage the successor must be able to promote organizational distinctiveness and be able to articulate its identity while keeping internal power struggles to a minimum and providing psychological safety. During the mid-life stage, beyond guiding organizational growth, the successor should be able to articulate the organizational culture, maintain internal integration, initiate ongoing assessment, and perhaps allow functional internal struggles. With maturity/stagnation of the organization, successor qualities include the sponsorship of organizational self-examination and the selective promotion of innovation and experimentation while carefully monitoring key resources, maintaining morale, and providing psychological safety. In each stage the successor should also be sensitive to needed major changes and possible transformative transition.

When succession occurs during a major organization change or a planned transformation, the question becomes: "At which point in each of these processes should succession occur?" The companion question is: "Are other managers able and willing to perform some of the roles in the processes?" At the onset of these processes, then, who will be responsible for intelligence/scanning, who will interpret problems and predicaments and challenge the system, who will be "godfather" and "lobbyist"? Thereafter, the roles necessary in each process differ, but again the question is whether the successor or someone else be responsible for performing them. At minimum, the general common roles noted above (i.e., cultural spokesman, rascal, etc.), are basic criteria for selection no matter when succession occurs.

The second general question asks if the succession event is anticipated or not, that is, was it planned for. The unanticipated replacement of executives, due either to surprise resignations, accidents, or the lack of succession planning, puts time pressures on the organization which tend to obscure consideration of relevant selection criteria.* The reason for succession and the disruption it causes differ. If anticipated even to some degree, the organization is more likely to have identified an appropriate reservoir of successor talent. Pertinent is whether this reservoir has been formed and/or is structured in terms of change and transformation competencies.

---

* Sometimes, of course, executives are simply removed. Weiner (1984) argues that such removals mostly serve a "scapegoating" function. While poor organizational performance usually is the result of many factors out of the CEO's control, the belief of CEO power and outcome impact leads to the CEO's termination when organizational performance is poor. The resulting catharsis then permits the subsequent succession process to be less loaded with negative affect.

The third question, i.e., who should be involved, focuses attention on the actors involved in succession. Some one or set of persons has to decide that a successor needs to be selected, to plan the selection process, to search for potential candidates, to choose the successor, and to see to it that appropriate socialization of the executive selected takes place. The first and third of these stages is always a line responsibility. The other steps may or may not also involve staff personnel—but always under the scrutiny of top management and directors, if there are any. In dynamic contexts the involvement of outsiders appears especially useful. If a consultant or external researcher exists who understands the organization and has a good ongoing relationship with top management, they may help by facilitating the selection process and providing expertise. The function of the outsider is primarily to ensure that a broad perspective is maintained and to help those responsible in confronting the dynamic realities of the succession context—functions that are difficult for those intimately involved to accomplish. Search for candidates is also helped by outsiders. While external search is commonly assisted by professional executive recruitment services, outsiders are often overlooked, foolishly, in internal searches. This is remarkable since outsiders are often involved in the assessing and developing of the internal talent pool.

Executive Development

Selection is most likely to succeed when the right person is available. This brings us to the matter of executive development. Internal talent pools come about through recruitment, formal development programs, and ongoing developmental experiences. Managerial recruitment during or in anticipation of major organizational change or transformation might use the roles identified earlier as the basis for screening prospective management candidates. Development programs for dynamic contexts should focus on health and personal development, of course, but should incorporate agendas related to team-building skill, change and transformation processes, organizational design, strategy formulation, cultural assessment, and issues in the future and in the general society that will possibly impinge on the organization. Several ongoing developmental experiences, pertinent for managers who will become candidates in an executive succession pool, are these: coaching and mentoring experiences, especially as the coach or mentor; assignments and projects that really stretch a manager's capabilities, that foster consulting and facilitation skills, and which require broad organizational assessment and diagnosis; activities that require building internal and external professional networks, and the development and use of others as sounding boards (i.e., "shadow" consultants, Schroder, 1974); and, responsible involvement in change and transformation events.

Concluding Remarks

This essay has argued that contemporary organizational environments are evermore changeful and impactful; that the reality of organizational life, therefore, is mostly one of change and transition; that organizations as dynamic contexts—either as moving through the stages of the organizational life cycle or as experiencing organizational change and transformation—give prominence to executive change and transition roles; and, that these roles thus provide the criteria for assessing executive behavior, selecting executive successors, and developing desirable executive competencies.

The essay has been exploratory in that considerations of dynamic contexts have heretofore been relatively underdiscussed, especially so for executive succession. No doubt as further inquiry into these areas proceeds, the preliminary conceptual frameworks provided here will be both refined and altered. They do, however, allow the work of understanding executive succession under dynamic, changeful conditions to begin in earnest. Initially these frameworks can serve to order and differentiate those descriptive studies and surveys that now exist. Hopefully, too, this essay will stimulate inquiry into the mechanisms by which these general considerations are translated into effective practices in particular organizations and industries. It is clear that the multiple considerations of executive succession in dynamic contexts contain many challenges for both organization scholars and management practitioners alike.

Craig C. Lundberg is Professor of Management and Organization, School of Business Administration, University of Southern California. He is the editor of the Organizational Behavior Teaching Review. *His current scholarly interests revolve around organizational culture, change roles and strategies, alternative modes of inquiry, and designing processes. His self perception is of a rancher, poet, lover, skier, applied behavioral scientist and gentle reformer of all systems of which he is a member.*

REFERENCES

Argyris, C., and Schon, D. A. *Organizational learning: A theory of action perspective.* Reading, MA: Addison-Wesley, 1978.

Bateson, G. *Mind and Nature: A necessary unity.* New York: Dutton, 1979.

Beckhard, R., and Harris, R. T. *Organizational transitions: Managing complex change.* Reading, MA: Addison-Wesley, 1977.

Browne, P. C., Vancil, R. F., and Sathe, V. "Cummins Engine Company," Harvard Business School Case 9-182-264, 1982.

Cameron, K., and Whetten, D. Perception of organization effectiveness across organization life cycles. *Administrative Science Quarterly,* **26,** 1981, 525–544.

Davis, S. M. *Managing corporate culture.* Cambridge, MA: Ballinger, 1984.

Dyer, W. G. Jr. Cultural evolution in organizations: The case of a family owned firm. Unpublished doctoral dissertation, Sloan School of Management, Massachusetts Institute of Technology, 1984.

Filley, A. C. A theory of small business and divisional growth. Unpublished doctoral dissertation, The Ohio State University, 1962.

Fombrun, C. J., Tichy, N. M., and Devanna, M. A. *Strategic human resource management*. New York: Wiley, 1984.

Frost, P. J., Moore, L. F., Louis, M. R., Lundberg, C. C., and Martin, J. (Eds.) *Organizational culture*. Beverly Hills: Sage, 1985.

Galbraith, J. R. Leadership and innovating organizations. Paper presented at the Academy of Management Meetings, San Diego, 1985.

Goodman, P. S., Bazerman, M., and Colon, E. Institutionalization of planned organizational change. In B. M. Staw and L. L. Cummings (Eds.), *Research in organizational behavior*, Vol. 2, Greenwich, CT: JAI Press, 1980.

Grusky, O. Administration succession in large organizations. *Social Forces*, **39**, 1960, 105–115.

Kanter, R. M. The architecture of organizational change: Linking micro-innovations to macro-transformation. Paper presented at the annual meeting of the Academy of Management, San Diego, August 1985.

Kilmann, R. H. *Beyond the quick fix: Managing five tracks to organizational success*. San Francisco: Jossey-Bass, 1984.

Kilmann, R. H., Saxton, M. J., Serpa, R., and Associates. *Gaining control of the corporate culture*. San Francisco: Jossey-Bass, 1985.

Kimberly, J. R. Issues in the creation of organizations: Initiation, innovation, and institutionalization. *Academy of Management Journal*, **22**, 1979, 437–457.

Kimberly, J. R., and Miles, R. H. *The organizational life cycle*. San Francisco: Jossey-Bass, 1980.

Kimberly, J. R., and Quinn, R. E. *Managing organizational transitions*. Homewood, IL: Irwin, 1984.

Lundberg, C. C. Toward a contextual model of human resource strategy: Lessons from the Reynolds Corporation. *Human Resource Management*, 1985a, **24**(1), 91–112.

Lundberg, C. C. On the feasibility of cultural intervention in organizations. In P. Frost, L. Moore, M. Louis, C. Lundberg, and J. Martin (Eds.), *Organizational culture*. Beverly Hills: Sage, 1985b.

Martin, J., Sitkin, S. B., and Boem, M. Founders and the elusiveness of a cultural legacy. In P. Frost, L. Moore, M. Louis, C. Lundberg, and J. Martin (Eds.), *Organizational culture*. Beverly Hills: Sage, 1985.

Mason, R., and Mitroff, I. I. *Challenging strategic planning assumptions*. New York: Wiley, 1981.

Miller, D., and Friesen, P. H. Archtypes of organizational transition. *Administrative Science Quarterly*, **25**, 1980, 268–299.

Mirvis, P. H. Managing research while researching managers. In P. Frost, L. Moore, M. Louis, C. Lundberg, and J. Martin (Eds.), *Organizational culture*. Beverly Hills: Sage, 1985.

Mohrman, A. M., and Lawler, E. E. III. The diffusion of QWL as a paradigm shift. Working Paper G81-13, Center for Effective Organizations, University of Southern California, 1983.

Nystrom, P., and Starbuck, W. H. To avoid organizational crises, unlearn *Organizational Dynamics*, **3**, 1984, 53–65.

Pfeffer, J. Power and resource allocation in organizations. In B. M. Staw and G. R. Salancik (Eds.), *New directions in organizational behavior*. Chicago: St. Clair Press, 1977.

Pfeffer, J. Management as symbolic action: The creation and maintenance of organizational paradigms. In L. Cummings and B. Staw (Eds.), *Research in organizational behavior*. Vol. 3, Greenwich, CT: JAI Press, 1981.

Pettigrew, A. On studying organizational cultures. *Administrative Science Quarterly*, **24**, 1979, 570–581.

Quinn, J. B. *Strategies for change: Logical incrementalism.* Homewood, IL: Irwin, 1980.

Schein, E. H. *Organizational culture and leadership.* San Francisco: Jossey-Bass, 1985.

Schon, D. A. *The reflective practitioner.* New York: Basic Books, 1983.

Schroder, M. The shadow consultant. *Journal of Applied Behavioral Science*, **10**, 1974.

Siehl, C. After the founder: An opportunity to manage culture. In P. Frost, L. Moore, M. Louis, C. Lundberg, and J. Martin (Eds.), *Organizational culture.* Beverly Hills: Sage, 1985.

Starbuck, W. H. *Organizational growth and development.* New York: Penguin Books, 1971.

Tichy, N., and Ulrich, D. Revitalizing organizations: The leadership role. In J. R. Kimberly and R. E. Quinn (Eds.), *Managing organizational transitions.* Homewood, IL: R. D. Irwin, 1984.

Turnstall, W. B. Breakup of the Bell system: A case study in cultural transformation. In R. H. Killmann, M. Saxton, and R. Serpa (Eds.), *Gaining control of the corporate culture.* San Francisco: Jossey-Bass, 1985.

Watzlawick, P., Weaklund, J. H., and Fisch, R. *Change: Principles and problem formulation.* New York: W. W. Norton, 1974.

Weick, K. *The social psychology of organizing* (2nd ed.). Reading, MA: Addison-Wesley, 1979.

Weick, K. The significance of corporate culture. In P. Frost, L. Moore, M. Louis, C. Lundberg, and J. Martin (Eds.), *Organizational culture.* Beverly Hills: Sage, 1985.

Weiner, N. Executive succession: An examination of the resource dependence model. *Canadian Journal of Administrative Sciences*, **1**, 1984, 321–337.

Heroes in Collision: Chief Executive Retirement and the Parade of Future Leaders

The exit and legacy of leaders can have an impact which rivals the reign of a leader. While leaders' retirement is important to us all, we know little about its dynamics. This article is part of a large research project on 200 retiring leaders. Three core dimensions of leaders' retirement are discussed.

We commonly judge our leaders based on their record of accomplishment an its required behavior. Their record includes measures of the size, growth, and duration of their contribution. Their behavior is examined along such lines as courage, influence, originality, strength, compassion, and responsiveness in the face of challenge to their mission. Thus what leaders do and how they do it captures our attention. There are also career issues regarding the reign of these people, but they tend to be less well appreciated. It is true that we often track the rise of leaders through the biographies of heroes, but that is where the career monitoring often stops. The leader's career, of course, hardly ends with the assumption of an ultimate position of supremacy. Leaders' departures, in particular, are every bit as important to understand as their rise to power or the qualities of their reign. This importance can be felt on the level of the individual leader wrestling over if and when to retire, the relations between successive leaders on lower rungs of the hierarchical ladder, and finally, on the level of the community personified by this supreme leader.

These three dimensions can be thought of as three sets of tensions: 1) those within the leader; 2) those across generations of leaders; and 3) those between leaders and their constituents. Thus, leaders' departures

* Professor Sonnenfeld acknowledges the helpful advise provided on the preparation of this manuscript by Ms. Cynthia Ingols, and Professors John P. Kotter, Howard H. Stevenson, Andrall Pearson, Walter J. Salmon, Joseph L. Bower, and Hugo Uyterhoven of the Harvard Business School, as well as Professors John Kimberly and Stewart Friedman of the Wharton School, and Mr. Harry Bernhard of IBM.

require the consideration of three sets of distinct tensions. This article will examine each of these tensions by looking first at the personal retirement dilemma, next the succession struggle across generations, and finally at the community's need for a smooth transition between leaders. The underlying tension on each of these levels is the need to balance justice for individual older leaders, the ambitions of younger leaders, and communities' needs for a leadership portfolio. If our goals are only to secure the opportunities of rising talent through turnover, we can waste the accumulated wisdom of the reigning leaders. If our goals are only the preservation in office of capable leaders through continuity, regardless of tenure and age, we can waste the energy and imagination of a whole generation of future leaders. The need to study leaders' retirement on these three levels is especially important when we look at chief executives today.

Retirement is a difficult event for all of us regardless of our occupation, but it is especially troublesome for institutional leaders. For leaders, retirement may be confession of their limits in life and hence represents the loss of the optimism so essential to all life. The fear of lost health, vitality, and one of life's centralities—work—threatens one's own belief in the future. The desperate determined clutching onto the throne by an aging ruler may deny other potential leaders of a future as well as deny society the experience of alternate leaders. A leader who frustrates goals of his or her followers will lose their support—hence lose the legitimacy of his or her reign. As visionaries, leaders become identified with the plan of the institution they lead. Their tenure and departure involves more than their personal fate: it involves the fate of the community. The transition between leaders can be so tumultuous that the community may lose its collective sense of direction. The departure of a leader involves unique responsibilities for this figure and a special interest by parties both inside and outside of the organization.

Changing demographic patterns suggest that constructive retirement programs in general and leadership succession in particular have begun to absorb more American public attention. The growing size of the older population will give increased muscle to those older executives who feel that they are being strongarmed out of productive mainstream roles. Now larger than 24 million people, the over-65 age sector of the American public is growing twice as fast as the rest of the population. Since 1950, it has doubled; this age group has grown by a fourth in the 1970s alone. By the year 2040, this population will double again to 55 million. Older Americans will comprise 18% of the population by then, up over 100% from the current 8%. The over-75 age group has grown ten-fold since 1900, while the over-85 crowd has grown 17 times since the turn of the century. In fact, by 1990, as the baby boom crosses midlife, there will be more Americans over 55 than of primary school age for the first time in history. The median age will grow from roughly 31 in 1985 to about 39 in the year 2040 (U.S. Bureau of Census, 1977).

As our American society has aged, the public spotlight has rotated to the activities of older people. Artists, diplomats, entertainers, politicians, and business leaders have become prominent symbols of late career vitality. They often battle decaying health, hostile societal attitudes, and personal doubts to remain connected to events. The continued contribution through their lifelong professions becomes a struggle. Maintaining one's involvement is only one of a number of struggles at this age. Equally compelling is the desire to preserve one's reputation accumulated over a career. Thus, in addition to seeking opportunities, older people must balance how to preserve their own individual integrity and how to best time their exit from their work organizations.

I. TENSIONS WITHIN THE LEADER: THE PERSONAL RETIREMENT DECISION

Holding on for Dear Life

Late career exit quandaries are resolved through various degrees of continuity in one's job. Some maintain their career full-throttle until the engines of life just give out. Others withdraw gradually and pursue other career interests. Still others scale back their involvement in the same career and allow more time for leisure. Finally, there are those who completely disengage and become disinterested in occupational life. One's health, personality, family needs, and array of opportunities dictate the likely amount of energy for one's career late in life.

In addition to this cluster of determinants is one's occupation itself. An occupation provides a peer group for reference to identify cultural expectations about what a person should do at a given age and also provides a network of empathic cohorts. Research on age grading suggests that expectations vary significantly among types of careers (Lawrence, 1984). Consider how ballerinas, boxers, and baseball players retire at half the age of judges, legislators, and actors. Notions of what characterizes glamorous new directions will vary by what sort of jobs are valued within an occupation. The pace of promotion and timing of exit will also vary across jobs, firms, and industries. An occupation also provides one with a certain pool of late life resources. Some tedious repetitive jobs may offer few skills and energies for later usage. Other occupations which are more intellectually, socially, or technically involving work may offer a great source of accomplishment, group membership, and purpose. Leaders, as an occupational class, can become both attached to their public exposure and their public impact. These conditions disappear with retirement.

Therefore, public figures such as performers, politicians, and corporate leaders may possess common work addictive qualities as occupations which demand great sacrifice of personal life and a consequent lifetime devotion to work. This may then make their withdrawal from work an especially unfulfilling event. The constant public scrutiny is intrusive, but it may also cause celebrities to become reliant upon the public's recognition of their community contribution. Let's consider a few examples of celebrities who are captured by the need to continue to perform. The great pianist Claudio Arrau continued playing 60 concerts a year at age 83. On approaching age 80 he revealed his philosophy of late career engagement:

> I am still under the illusion that I play about a hundred concerts a season, but I don't think its quite a reality anymore. Maybe its between eighty and a hundred concerts. I don't want to cut down at all. (Horowitz, 1984, p. 187)

When asked why he is unwilling to reduce his commitments he responded:

> Because its a question of giving in to age without reason. If I felt weak, that would be a reason. On the contrary, I get strength from performing, but everyone wants to protect me. (Horowitz, 1984, p. 189)

Another octogenarian, Ruth Gordon, expressed a similar philosophy shortly before her death. She first debuted on Broadway in 1915 and continued on stage and screen as well as writing until her death in 1985. She died at age 88 with four new films about to be released. She offered this explanation on her insistence on continued activity, "If you live long enough, you are your work and your work is you" (Gussow, 1985). Representative Claude Pepper, the 86-year-old chairman of the House Rules Committee has enjoyed a colorful political career which has spanned 46 years in both houses of Congress and nine presidents. He also has claimed to draw strength from his continued contribution: "I'm like an old hickory tree. The older I get, the tougher I get (Perry, 1982).

Turning to the executive suite, we find many ready examples of the same career longevity. For example, consider the following: Armand Hammer, who has run Occidental Petroleum for 29 years, is 88 years old; 74-year-old William Norris has run Control Data for 29 years; J. Peter Grace, 73 years old, has run W. R. Grace for 41 years; or 85 year old Florence Eiseman who has overseen the manufacture of stylish clothing bearing her name since 1931.

Perhaps most noteworthy was the Cleveland industrial empire builder Cyrus Eaton, who died at age 95 as chairman of the Chesapeake and Ohio Railroad and as a director of Detroit Steep Rock Iron Mines, The Baltimore and Ohio Railroad, Cleveland-Cliffes Iron Co., the Kansas City Power and Light Company, and the Sherwin Williams Company; as owner and operator of two large cattle farms; as trustee of eight institutions including the University of Chicago, and Denison University, and as a fellow of the American Academy of Arts and Sciences. Another long-tenured chief executive—Justin W. Dart, who built Dart Industries, a diversified consumer products and chemical company, out of a struggling drugstore chain called United-Rexall Drugs. Dart had announced at age 72, "I want my death and my retirement to be simultaneous" (Hollie, 1979). Three years later, having merged his company with Kraft Inc., and subsequently serving as chairman of the new corporation's executive committee, he died. At age 70, Ben W. Heineman, the chairman of Northwest Industries, shelved his initial retirement plans to perform a major corporate overhaul. In accepting a three year extension, he explained "I'm not ready to retire from life. I'm not going to sit around with a blanket over my knees" (Johnson, 1983). Two years later, still with no clear successor identified, his company was acquired by Chicago investor William F. Farley. In these examples, we see the fierce spirit of determination of highly prominent people who are anxious not to abdicate their earned positions while they are alive and their health is still strong. Like other public figures, corporate leaders can become absorbed in their prominent roles. The attention and feedback can be wearing for some, but many find it energizing. Unlike other public figures, they become accustomed to having direct influence over their constituency. The loss of attention and influence is more intense for corporate leaders than most other occupations. Thus we see many resisting retirement.

Quitting While Ahead

There are many prominent older people who take a dramatically opposing position to this struggle to cling to one's job for dear life. Eric Hoffer, the author and social critic, died in 1983, at the age of 80, three months after receiving the Presidential Medal of Freedom. Born in 1902 and partially blind until he was 15 years old, Hofer spent 23 years as a migrant worker on farms and in mines. He worked as a longshoreman until age 65. Among his nine books was the blockbuster entitled *The True Believer*, published in 1951. In 1970, at the age of 68, he withdrew from public life, resigned as a lecturer at the University of California at Berkeley, quit his newspaper column, and terminated his formerly frequent television appearances. He explained that this decision was based on his observations that "Any man can ride a train, only a wise man knows when to get off" (Turner, 1983). Hoffer was disturbed as he had found himself becoming increasingly labeled a reactionary by the "counterculture" activities of the 1960s that challenged his stands on issues such as the Vietnam War. Hoffer decided to leave the public eye with his reputation, his privacy, and his dignity intact. Longevity might only erode a lifetime of accomplishment.

Rather than minimize the erosion of a professional reputation, some seniors may seek retirement to escape from the overexhaustion and overexposure common to public figures. Eighty-five year old actress Helen Hayes commented on her attitude on turning 80 and on her career which began at age six:

> Time was when I proudly declined an arm offered to help me up and down a step. Now I tend to grab for it. I used to comply smilingly when asked sometimes in the middle of a meal for an autograph. Already I've begun to snarl. I shall refuse any longer to be the fount of wisdom on how to launch a career in everything from acting to rose growing . . . In brief, I'm casting off the shackles of celebrity. (Hayes, 1980)

Her defiance to remain engaged and locked in the same role with the public is in marked contrast to those described earlier, such as Ruth Gordon, who were delighted to become captured by their work.

Many business leaders also feel that they must avoid having their personal existence defined by their job. Sigmund Warburg has warned that business leaders have responsibilities to leave the stage even more compelling than those of other public performers. The founder of S. G. Warburg and Co., the prominent merchant bankers of London, he declared that he wanted to retire before his doctor said that he must. After beginning his career at N. M. Rothschild and Sons in London, he trained in Boston with Lybrand, Ross, Montgomery, and with Kuhn Loeb and Co. in New York. In 1930, he opened the Berlin office of M. M. Warburg, the ancient influential merchant bank of Hamburg. Four years later, he fled the Nazi's murderous rampage for London to begin a new life. The proud firm founded by Moses Marcus Warburg in 1798 with direct roots back to the 16th century was taken over by the Nazis. In 1934, with less than $5000 to his name, Sigmund rebuilt a great deal of the strength of the old Warburg firm. On reaching age 63 in 1963, he felt that the organization should make him dispensable:

> Leaders in industry and finance are often inclined not to step down before the decline of their capabilities becomes manifest, holding on too long to their positions and thus preventing the formation of a strong chain of potential successors. . . . Thus I am convinced that stepping down will not weaken but on the contrary will strengthen our group. (Wechsberg, 1966)

Thus, prominent figures such as corporate leaders may escape their exhausting routine and responsibilities to the public through retiring. Those who leave office enthusiastically may meet both societal and personal needs for renewal.

So far, we have argued that retirement is difficult for all, but especially trying for public figures. We considered the perspective of those who refuse to give in to age and retire as well as the perspective of those who believe in stepping out of the spotlight. In addition to this loss of attention, however, leaders must sacrifice something far greater. While any public figure can lose an audience through retirement, the retired leader loses the power to shape that audience. This power is the reward, for some, of a lifetime struggle against threatening authorities and treacherous peers. Additionally, in retiring, leaders find that their dreams have hit a ceiling never before reached. Their personal ambitions have been furthered by persuading constituents to accept the leader's dreams as a community possession. Leaders' retirements require them to acknowledge the rejection of a personal dream. In the next section we will examine the role of dreams in leaders and the conflict of dreams across generations.

The personal dilemma all older leaders face—to hold on or to quit—is fraught with dangers on each side. People who choose to hold on claim that they maintain their strength and energy through continued performance. They continue to command attention and hold power. Indeed, it seems their individual needs are well served. On the other hand, those who chose to retire speak of other themes. These leaders want to maintain reputations they built in their prime. Some speak of the primacy of the interests of the community over their own continued reign and the interests of succeeding generations of leaders. For the leader to have gained office, it was critical to be able to sell oneself to a community. To do this, the leader must meet the community's need for a sustaining vision. Thus, the leader must believe in his or her own immortality. Ultimately, we may pose this maintenance of performance vs. maintenance of reputation as two avenues for individual immortality—one through continued personal presence and the other through the organizational legacy.

II. TENSIONS ACROSS GENERATIONS OF LEADERS:
OPPORTUNITIES FOR SUCCESSORS

Boulevard of Broken Dreams

Psychoanalytic theorist Daniel Levinson has argued that leaders over age 65 create career plateaus down the line through their mere existence and thus retard the development of future leaders. Levinson thought late-aged executives should leave office, stating that if the leaders does not leave,

> . . . he is 'out of phase' with his own generation and
> he is in conflict with the generation of middle adulthood
> who need to assume greater responsibilities . . . even

> when a man has a high level of energy and skill he is ill-
> advised to retain power into late adulthood. He tends to
> be an isolated leader in poor touch with his followers
> and overly idealized or hated by them. The continuity of
> the generations is disrupted. (Levinson et al., 1978)

The leaders responsible for grooming future leaders can therefore spiritually sabotage their own executive development programs. If the company's mission no longer includes the fulfillment of his or her dreams, why then work to fulfill the collective dreams of the company? Misery does not just love company, it loves miserable company. A boss filled with despair over his or her own lethargic career may be a destructive mentor. The grand fanfare designed to excite and cultivate new leaders can aggravate the resentment of lost opportunity. New high potential designers appear as threatening rivals. Training for longer-term payouts is discouraged with an emphasis on the present. Bosses thus warn subordinates to meet today's performance and leave the career dreaming for later. Initiative is dismissed as foolish naivete. Ambition becomes seen as opportunism.

This jealousy by the old is translated by the intended protégés as selfishness and stodginess. Vast reservoirs of accumulated wisdom remain untapped as the young seek to bypass those who obstruct the free flow of the career stream. Instead of being perceived as valuable reservoirs of learning, older superiors can be seen as dangerous rapids to circumnavigate. This intergenerational hostility only intensifies as the manager realizes that he or she is perceived as merely a hindrance to the careers of others. The response is to intensify the campaign to prove one's centrality and ensure survival—thus perpetuating the cycle.

The tensions across generations are based upon the premise that we can take the full continuum of work ages and divide it into homogeneous clusters. Just as mass society has been segmented into twenty-year epochs, so can the members of specific institutions be. Researchers across disparate fields reach uncommon agreement in acknowledging the profound differences of interest at early, mid, and late career. Some believe the differences are based on our interactions with the changing opportunities and challenges. This sociological research has identified the vastly different role expectations imposed upon us as we assume different positions of responsibility over time (Schein, 1971; Hall, 1976; Miller and Form, 1951; Pelz and Andrews, 1966; Lawrence, 1984). Other researchers, more psychological in nature, have looked at life stage tasks which we must master as we age. Changing relationships and changing biological conditions require more than altered work tasks (Jacques, 1965; Jung, 1933; Erikson, 1963; Vaillant, 1977).

The more internal distinctions across generations have to do with different stages of evolving life structures. This concept of the life structure is the overall design of a person's life at a given time. Personal priorities change as we redefine our existence relative to our jobs, family, friendships, health, and wider society. The changes we experience do not have a mere transitory impact. Rather, their force is cumulative. We gain greater personal insight, recognize hidden limits, and appreciate obscured strengths. Confidence over different life sectors shifts and personal priorities are rearranged accordingly.

Looking first at adulthood, we see an impatience to escape the shadows of adolescence through the pursuit of dreams of adult life. By mid-life these dreams may be reformulated. Many people reappraise the barriers within which we exist. Later, we struggle to create a legacy which will survive us. By the 50s, we work on implementing this plan more through cautious fine tuning rather than the major reformulation of our commitments as we have in our 40s. In late adult life, the last vestiges of youth forever disappear. There are numerous societal pressures to disengage from work and accept less central assignments. A deep reappraisal of the entirety of one's life begins.

These external and internal forces lead to different clusters of interests for early, mid, and late career managers. In early career, membership, advancement, training, challenge, adventure, and the bright lights and loud trumpets of celebrity are important. We are anxious to get ahead and to distinguish ourselves from the pack. In midcareer, we seek new life goals, proof of maintained growth and respect, and are fearful of obsolescence. We move from the role of player to the role of coach. In late career, we weather the constant pressures of decline and withdrawal. The tensions across these generations grow as the pace of movement across each life stage by a generation seems to be the casualty of the greed of the other generations. The life patterns we see around us are frightening because they are not completely under our own control. The old represent future erosion of power and health. The young represent all the hope and vitality that's been lost.

After health, family, and friendships, the greatest of such personal losses is the loss of one's life dream. To Daniel Levinson, the life dream is at best only tenuously affixed in reality. It is a mixture of personalized images of one's self that has been developed in adolescence and projected into the adult world. Personal style, occupation roles, family relations, and community involvements are quite vague but underlying goals. By age 30, experience and mentors help us to clarify the goals which underlie this vision. As we move out of apprenticeship at work and into established positions at midlife, we come to see whether the dream has been attained. It is often reformulated now with the wisdom of adulthood to guide us.

By late career, this dream is either attained or attacked by the realities of accomplishments. The gloom of despair thickens as one realizes that advancing age may now preclude one from ever reaching life goals. The more central work is to one's life goals, the more painful retirement is to someone who feels unfulfilled by late career. Retirement comes to symbolize the forcible loss of a dream. At the same time, the review of one's record of achievement may provide one with a sense of contentment and satisfaction. The key is whether reachable goals have been met.

Saluting the Future by Purging the Past

If we thus conceive of effective leaders as those who, in part, serve as guides to community salvation, it is easy to see why workers, their managers, students of management, and society at large are all preoccupied with identifying future leaders. Business leaders are heroes to their own immediate constituencies—their employees, their owners, and their communities. We are interested in emerging leaders because they are symbols of the future. Autobiographies on the rise of presidents, generals, and corporate chieftains are almost as compelling and popular to general audiences as are the tales of such figures of Oddyseus, Beowulf, Samson, or Superman.

Similarly, our best modern executive development programs strive to locate and groom promising young stars drifting somewhere in the seas of management within large corporations. Succession planning, the development of subordinates, and fast track programs are the common activities used to identify and cultivate new leaders. The hidden message of many of these programs is that executive development stops at midcareer: you are out of the tournament once you begin to stagnate in a position. Pre-retirement counseling, ample pensions, and retiree clubs are growing to ease the exit out of leadership roles. Late-career switches into new fields are not commonly seen as shrewd investments within firms. Such changes generally require the older person to leave the firm to locate new opportunities.

Many firms facing career system problems such as log jams in the promotion streams or a dramatic retrenchment crisis have turned to early retirement incentive programs as the most humane and least disruptive option. Career stagnation and massive layoffs have been minimized or even averted through such voluntary severance programs. Firms such as IBM, Polaroid, DuPont, Uniroyal, Crown Zellerbach, Firestone, Metropolitan Life, Sears Roebuck, B. F. Goodrich, A&P, Eastman Kodak, Travelers Insurance, American Can, Pan Am, American Airlines, and United Airlines are among those who have successfully thinned their ranks through fair and attractive early retirement programs (Lubins and King, 1980; Darby, 1982).

Despite the lucrative lure of the programs, firms have been astounded by the stampede of workers enthusiastic about these programs. Following a 45% drop in profits in the first nine months of 1981, Polaroid designed an especially tempting exit program. It encouraged the exit of 934 employees, 7.2% of the domestic work force, well in excess of the 6% target. On average, the departing workers were age 53.4 with 18.4 years of experience. All parties, participants, and nonparticipants reported that the program made them feel more positive about the future of the company (Kochan and Barucci, 1985). Several key employees left, such as the top marketing executive and an heir to the presidency. Nonetheless, the firm was sufficiently pleased: it renewed the program four years later. Similarly, lagging sales growth and an unfavorable report on employee productivity relative to competitors led DuPont in 1985 to prune "deadwood." In the spring, company chairman Edward Jefferson announced a program which encouraged 12,000 early retirements, or a shocking 8% of its work force. This was twice the projection of 6000 departures, with the company losing some of those it had hoped to keep. Gaps in some places required the hiring of less experienced workers (Freedman, 1985). Senior management, about 800 people, were excluded from the program. The company estimated that the program would save $230 million after taxes the next year.

Thus, the none too subtle presumptions guiding such tradeoffs of the careers of older workers for the careers of younger workers are that:

1) Younger workers with longer remaining work lives present a wiser investment in the future. Freeing up positions to those next in line provides opportunities for others to grow and creates incentives for ambitious workers.
2) Younger workers are less costly than older workers when we consider their lower wage and benefit requirements for comparable performance.
3) The retirement of older workers relieves the organization of incompetence and complacency.
4) When thinning the ranks becomes a necessity, the retirement of older workers, with fewer dependents and consequently fewer financial pressures, is easier than laying off younger workers with younger families and possibly greater hardships.

There are counter perspectives on each issue:

1) It can be argued that younger workers, with their lower work commitment, and higher turnover, are a less reliable investment in the future of the firm. Older workers, with longer company length of service, already demonstrate a greater sorting out of "leavers" and "stayers."
2) The higher absenteeism, greater tardiness, and performance lag during start-up time for younger workers suggests that they may not always be a bargain purchase (Schein, 1964). We know much less about the skills, interests, and motivation of younger workers. Any increased overt costs must be compared against the hidden costs of younger workers. Furthermore, these costs can be compared to the price of loyalty, cultural commitment, and better performance records.

3) The assumptions of lower competence and complacency are predicated on a faulty correlation between age and job performance. The research universally suggests a bimodal distribution of performance over time with a striking drop at midlife, but peaks in one's thirties and fifties (Sonnenfeld, 1978). Certain jobs requiring less physical dexterity and speed such as those which favor experience based judgment and persuasion are often better filled by older workers.

4) Finally, the notion of justice behind exiting older workers rather than younger workers is contradictory to the original premises of seniority-based traditions of job security. Paternalistic masters of servile laborers had rewarded those who gave their youth as dedicated laborers. Later, large industry seniority rules were introduced in the railroads and printing trades at the turn of the century. The goal was to allow employers as well as employees to circumvent corrupt and capricious foreman who sold jobs for cash, private labor, or sexual favors (Mater, 1939). Legally imposed collective bargaining through the Wagner Act of 1935 helped spread this protection of older workers. Merit being equal, the worker with longer service was to be retained (Senate Comm. on Educ. and Labor, 1939; Marquart and McDowell, 1944). The preference towards older workers was seen as the safest means of seeking justice in personnel priorities. Even today, courts have supported seniority claims over other claims of employment protection such as affirmative action (Wermiel, 1985). Some research has also suggested that the exit of more senior, older workers will not lead to the creation of opportunities for younger workers as the position vacated often disappears with the incumbent (Bernstein, 1965).

Whether biased or just, the results of these programs are impressive. Workers display overwhelmingly favorable responses to these voluntary retirement programs. Further consideration of who leaves early and why they are leaving early can reveal that these buyout programs often attract those seeking an escape from a deadend job. Surveys on the attitudes of managers towards retirement suggest that financial concerns have a great deal to do with their retirement plans (Jud, 1981). In fact, financial considerations have been found by most researchers to have a greater influence upon retirement decisions than such important other influences as one's health or family considerations (Pyron and Greene, 1969). Appropriately, most early retirement programs offer especially attractive financial incentives. The 1982 program at Polaroid, for example, offered up to two and a half years of full pay after departure. The scaling of exit rewards depended on seniority with the firm.

Those opting for such lucrative programs can use the funds to invest in new careers. Workers frequently report perceptions of reduced opportunities in their firm with increasing age (Jud, 1981). Follow-up research on one major employer's recent early retirement program identified equal portions of those who felt "pushed" out of the firm through unsatisfactory job conditions as those who were "pulled" by the lure of other career options (Smith, 1980). In both cases, career opportunity was an important precipitating condition.

While some may volunteer to leave work feeling that their career situation drove them to retirement, others who elect to defer retirement seem to have more intellectually involving job conditions (Sonnenfeld, 1978; McConnell, 1983). White collar professional and more senior managers seem far less interested in early retirement than physical laborers with more routine jobs. This reluctance towards retiring was demonstrated in a survey of 200 recently retired chief executives and presidents of Fortune 500 firms (Johnston and Lannamann, 1984):

- 60% had returned to work within two years,
- 87% of these executives had returned within six months of their original retirement,
- 33% were working fulltime.

Personal satisfaction and a sense of accomplishment were the main justifications these retired leaders provided. Top corporate leaders with exciting careers, little financial needs, and strong desires to remain active are not likely to have the same attraction to lucrative retirement packages. For example, after his retirement at age 67, entrepreneur James A. Ryder declined a $200,000 a year payment not to compete with his old firm, Ryder Leasing (Sales and Marketing Management, 1981). By the time he was 70 years old, he had gone on to create Jartran and built it into a $100 million rival company. Over 40 years, Ryder had built his firm Ryder Systems into a $1 billion firm. He stated that the only reason he had left originally was that he had lost control over his outsider dominated board (Sales and Marketing Management, 1981). Earlier in this article, we reviewed some examples of well known firms run by leaders in their 80s and 90s. These leaders have either triumphed societal prejudice and should be applauded or they have ignored society's pleas and should be relieved of office. Since we are so consumed by our search for new leaders, we fail to distinguish constructive from destructive patterns of departing leaders.

Agitation Across Generations

In various subtle ways, however, we do distinguish leaders' retirements from those of others. For example, our current legislation suggests an eagerness to allow companies to retire top executives earlier than other workers. Some top executives are subject to mandatory retirement at age 55, 60, and 65. The Old Age Discrimination Employment

Act of 1978, which extended mandatory retirement to age 70 plus (and the revision in 1984), exempted from protection key corporate policymakers who qualify for pensions above $44,000. Beyond the dangers associated with the community consequences of the failing individual judgment of these leaders, what is of special concern lies in two forms of intergenerational conflict which pit predecessors and successor against each other for the role of incumbent. One form of conflict is rooted in the conflict of interest across cohorts based on struggles for opportunity and resources. The other form is less political and more personal. It is based upon the awareness of one's aging and unmet dreams.

People who experience common events simultaneously tend to share perceptions of the event. Thus, a generation as a group of people who have shared wars, depressions, political assassinations, demographic shifts, technological breakthroughs, and the like, share the lingering influences of these events upon beliefs and actions. The power of marker events and patterns of communication within a cohort lead to the imprinting of social values (Hyman, 1954; Crittendon, 1962; Eisenstadt, 1956; Elden, 1973). A group of leaders sharing both societal experiences and company histories will tend to converge on a ritualization of "how things are done." Innovative ideas and new top executives may not be greeted kindly by these executives, who may be angered by the shattering of their world view. Research has often cited the link between innovation and personnel changes (Miles and Snow, 1978). Newer research on turnover of corporate officers suggests that other cohorts drive out newly arriving top corporate officers from outside their cohort (Pfeffer, 1979; Wagner et al., 1984). These sorts of generational clashes represent interest groups in conflict. Like social class or an ethnic group, one's belonging does not rely upon agreement with fellow members. Instead, people are born into a generation and are magnetically drawn towards associates with common ideologies.

Such combat across generations is heightened when we allow for a more dynamic view of interest group tension. While membership in a generation does not rely upon the acceptance of other members—unlike other ascriptive interest groups, like ethnicity—we are forced to move from group to group by the common prodding of age. Thus, any balance across generations is perpetually upset. In particular, dramatic differences in the relative size of each generation affects the relative mix of personal opportunities. Demographers have noted the times in history when the populace was between the ages of 20 and 40. These times have been associated with great civil strife such as the French and American Revolutions, and the Protestant Reformation (Ryder, 1965). The young were viewed as engines driving social change with no allegiance to the past.

The same demographers have drawn parallels to the great youth unrest of the 1960s. Psychologists such as Kenneth Keniston, anthropologist Margaret Mead, and popular writers such as Charles Reich clamored to interpret the meaning of the cultural artifacts shared by this feisty generation (Kenisten, 1971, 1976; Reich, 1970). The common sentiment of such far ranging authors was that the college experience was a catalytic event in mobilizing one generation against the one which it followed. The age segregation of the campus brought together an interest group which had only suspected their shared frustration. The villain to this "counter-culture" was an intransigent culture of the generation in power.

As the post-war baby boom generation left campus, crowding continued into the workplace. By 1975, one-fourth of all people aged 25–29 had completed four or more years of college. This was a 50% increase over 1970. Between 1976 and 1985, 10.4 million college graduates competed for only 7.7 jobs traditionally held by college graduates. Accordingly, the economic value of these degrees in the workplace tumbled. College graduates earned 53% more than high school graduates in 1969, but by 1974 they were only earning 35% more. By 1980, college graduates crested at 1/3 of all 24-year-olds. By 1994, the number of 19–22 year olds (traditional college ages) will drop to about 25% of the 1980 peak. Thus, the demographic pressure for an expanding hierarchy is relaxing, leaving this baby boom cohort hanging out on a limb. The estimated return on each dollar invested in higher education has declined from 12% for graduates in the 1950s and 1960s to 8.5% for graduates of the 1970s (Natl. Committee for Manpower Policy Spec. Report, 1978; Freeman, 1976).

Thus, a gap between aspirations and realities is growing. The employment situation for this postwar cohort suggests one that is characterized by high education, lower initial wages, and diminished promotion opportunities. As they climb career ladders they will be hitting the ankles of the immobile incumbents above them. One social commentator who studied this generation's movement through life wrote,

> A generation that had expected to become chiefs will have to be braves. In effect, the entire generation will be like a large group of people being moved from a big room into a small room. Some will shove their way in, picking up bruises in the process; others will try to get in and fall; still more will not try at all. (Jones, 1980)

The career tension here is that each generation will see its own disappointment as a partial casualty of another generation's greed. The young complain of the burned out hulks which block their paths. The middle aged complain about the stodgy old-timers ahead and obnoxious opportunists behind. The old complain about the chain of impatient upstarts who seeks personal glory more than company contribution. Two centuries ago, Samuel Johnson said, "Every old man complains of the growing depravity of the world and the insolence of the rising generations." The old are resentful that their accumulated wisdom and years of dedicated service seem to count for so little to the young. They feel an implied message that their greatest contribution to the firm is to gracefully leave, regardless of the quality of their work. Thus, all ages discover that hard work and commitment do not guarantee the just rewards they had assumed would follow from early to late career. This discovery is unsettling: it leads to intergenerational scapegoating over the career frustrations of younger generations.

III. TENSIONS BETWEEN THE LEADER AND THE COMMUNITY: A SUCCESSION OF HEROES

Selecting Visions of the Future

Like a parade of marching bands passing the judges, our business executives can be viewed as a procession of passing generations. For a brief period, perhaps a decade or two, each generation enjoys displaying its finest effort before the reviewing stand. When the show is over, the band performs its rehearsed routines with less fervor as it marches on down the road. Organizations that survive and flourish across generations have succeeded in passing on the band major's baton from leader to leader of succeeding generations. While each generation has dreams of glories which are, in part, fueled by the inspiring visions of their leaders, it is the leader who directs the human formation behind which the individual performers follow. In addition, by setting the pace of the procession, the leader orchestrates the speed of his or her replacement in the spotlight.

Literature on business leadership celebrates the rise to power and accomplishments of incumbent leaders. The qualities of the next generation are intensively examined to be sure that the chain of triumphs will not be broken. Failing incumbents and flawed new candidates are valuable examples of nominations to be skillfully avoided in the future. Outgoing leaders, successful or not, are largely forgotten once departed. The spotlight moves to the new incumbents and their likely successors. Unlike other creatures, human beings are aware of tomorrow and anxious to be prepared for its arrival. The rising leader represents tomorrow for us today. Leaders bring us, among other managerial qualities, a prophetic vision. We struggle to shape the development of leaders in an effort to shape our future.

The leader then, much like a folk hero, offers to guide us with a new map of the future. The departing leader exits with his or her maps tucked away in a pocket, because successful or not, these maps represent only plans for the past. Society cares most about the history of the climb of leaders and their reign when it can provide lessons for future rulers. What lessons can there be, however, in the actual exit of the outgoing leader? The style of departure of a retiring leader has implica-

tions for the quality and depth of the internal pool of leaders, the continuity of accumulated executive wisdom, and the degree of human turbulence experienced by insiders and outsiders. Winston Churchill
warned in a speech to the House of Commons, "If we open a quarrel
between the past and the present, we shall find that we have lost the
future" (Churchill, 1940). Do we have the luxury of caring about departing leaders if there is so much to monitor in the rise of new leaders?

In the remainder of this article, we consider why leaders' ascents
capture the high beams while leaders' departures are left in shadows.
We will draw parallels between business leaders as visionaries in their
ability to deliver plans for the future.

Future Leaders and Future Visions

How a leader leaves office is as important to his or her constituents as
how the office is acquired. Nonetheless, our attention is not balanced
between these events. We hear regularly of the violent warfare surrounding prominent cases of corporate executive succession struggles,
yet that is where the discussion begins and ends. The collective wisdom
on leadership departures does not appear in best-selling management
guides, research reports, or classroom texts. Our classic literature on
leadership has been far more concerned with the ascent and contribution of leaders than with their descent (For an exemption, see Kotter,
1985). The making of presidents, the rise up the corporate hierarchy, the
effectiveness of top corporate leaders, the ethics of the top executives,
the genius of entrepreneurs, and the courage of turnaround experts
reflect the range of such frequent published discussions. The discussions of leadership have inspired the needed debate and programs
needed to spark revitalization of our institutions. These discussions,
however, reveal the common concern with the future that is shared by
society-at-large.

Evidence of our fascination with the future abounds. Consider our
daily thirst for meteorological forecasts for places we will not visit for
months or years. Similarly consider the continued popularity of modern
mysticism in our daily newspapers as evidenced through astrological
predictions and stock market projections. As computers replace crystal
balls, soothsaying has grown enormously. The World Future Society
now claims thirty thousand members. Respected universities offer degrees in a new discipline calling itself "futurology." Psychologist Robert
W. White long ago labeled this drive for preparatory information "competence motivation." This referred to efforts to master the complex uncertainties of a complex environment (White, 1959).

We are interested in the creation of leaders, however, because the
fortune tellers, however expert, are frequently wrong. The lack of consensus and failure to approximate major inflationary, employment, and

consumption patterns over the past decade has resulted in a drop in credibility for econometricians. Frequently there are as many economic forecasts as there are forecasters (McGinley, 1985). Business disaffection with such forecasting is best evidenced through the dismantling of siz-able econometric groups within major banks.

We thus turn to leaders in the hope that they will possess the qualities needed to guide us effectively through unknown trails which lie ahead. Recent books on corporate leadership highlight the leader's role as the corporate visionary. Donaldson and Lorsch's study of the top management of 12 Fortune 500 firms cautioned chief executives not to delegate the strategic vision to strategic planners. Contrary to popular notions, Lorsch and Donaldson found a striking long-term executive view of the destiny of their firms (Donaldson and Lorsch, 1985). Harry Levinson and Stuart Rosenthal's study of prominent chief executives concluded:

> Implicitly, but also often explicitly, these leaders saw themselves as having an obligation to society . . . They held out impossible goals and insisted they were going to achieve them . . . the leader must have a highly developed capacity for abstraction, for vision, and the strength to take charge. He must pull his organization into the future (Levinson and Rosenthal, 1984).

Richard Pascale and Anthony Athos called this contribution the creation of superordinate goals (Pascale and Athos, 1981). In their book, *Leaders*, Warren Bennis and Burt Nanus state:

> Leaders are the most results oriented individuals in the world and results get attention. Their visions or intentions are compelling and pull people toward them . . . like a child completely absorbed with creating a sand castle in a sand box, they draw others in (Bennis and Nanus, 1985).

The leaders provide a vision for the future and a road map telling us how to journey safety there. What does this tell us about the retirement of top leaders? If chief executives are lionized within their firms and given the status of living legends, we should consider their similarity to the contribution of actual folk heroes.

The Business of Heroes and the Heroes of Business

Today we frequently are glorifying business leaders into societal heroes. In fact, Bennis and Nanus go so far as to list such world shapers as Winston Churchill, Mahatma Ghandi, and Franklin Delano Roosevelt alongside such corporate titans as Thomas J. Watson (IBM), Edwin Land (Polaroid), and to identify Alfred P. Sloan (General Motors), Ray Kroc

(McDonalds), and Lee Iacocca (Chrysler) as similar visionary leaders (Bennis and Nanus, 1985). In emerging research on leadership, day-to-day management activities are deemphasized relative to broader agendas of action. The study of successful chief executives describes these figures by their longer-run heroic missions. Given this identification with folk heroes, it is appropriate to briefly examine what mythic figures contribute.

Functions of heroes include the demonstration of code of honor and most importantly, the deliverance from the dangers lurking in the future of turbulent cultures. Joseph E. Campbell's classic anthropological study of heroes across centuries, continents, and cultures has labeled the function of deliverance from future hazard the "monomyth" of the hero (Campbell, 1949: 30–31). For example, consider Campbell's summary of Virgil's Aeneid (IV):

> Aneas went down into the underworld, crossed the dreadful river of the dead, threw a sop to the three headed watchdog Corbus, and conversed, at last, with the shade of his dead father. All things were unfolded to him: the destiny of souls, the destiny of Rome, which he was to found, and in what ways he might endure every burden. (Campbell, 1949: 18)

We might consider heroic legends throughout the Old Testament, such as Joseph's interpretation of the Pharoh's dream or Moses' revelations, which led the people of Israel out of Egypt, a land of oppression, through the wilderness of the Sinai, to eventually receive the Tables of Law and to discover the Promised Land. The wisdom and leadership of Jesus, Mohammed, the Aztec god Tezcatlipoca, and other ancient heroes further characterize the leader as a dreamer who acts on the visions revealed. These leaders' dreams represent a concept of existence which is far more expansive than the mere enrichment of the dreamer's existence alone.

The hero is embraced not merely because he is a creative dreamer, but rather it is the contest and quality of the dream itself which helps to catapult the hero into prominence. This discussion challenges conventional cliches which distinguish between "dreamers" and "doers." It seems that society has embraced truly inspirational leaders who ascend to their heights by being dreamers who translate their hazy visions into concrete realities. But the quality of the heroic dream is different. The heroic dreamer does not succeed by conjuring simple self aggrandizing images. When society accepts the leader's heroic dream, it ceases to be a personal possession. The intimacy of a dream is lost as is the human identity of the dreamer. The creator of the dream becomes a symbol of the underlying vision. When the vision becomes passé, so, too, does the reign of the leader.

The retirement tension between leaders and their organizations derives from the possible rejection of their life mission by their constituency. It is not surprising, then, that chief executives have an especially challenging time with retirement. Their purpose and self worth have become increasingly tied into the well being of the firm; they have maneuvered to ensure that the expectations of their owners, workers, and neighbors were satisfactorily addressed, often at the expense of their own physical and psychological well being.

Succesion Struggles

Warburg's philosophy, expressed earlier, captures a sentiment shared by many admirals of industry, whether entrepreneurs of emerging firms or the reshapers of existing corporations. The cultivation of a successor and the actual transfer of power to the next executive is frequently considered one of leadership's greatest challenges. At the turn of the century, sociologist Max Weber referred to this transfer as the "institutionalization of charisma" (Weber, 1947) whereby the continuity of the organization beyond the life of the reigning personality is planned and actualized. Thirty years after Weber, chief executive and social theorist Chester Barnard underscored the continuous adaptation of the system as a fundamental function of the executive (Barnard, 1938). And yet another 30 years later, the relationship between leadership succession and firm adaptation was empirically supported in the pioneering work of sociologist Oscar Grusky, who found management succession to be an effective way to remedy organizational stagnation (Grusky, 1969). And research linking succession to financial performance has found that financially troubled firms have either very long-termed or very short-termed CEOs. Moderate terms are characteristic in financially healthy firms (Hambrick, 1985; Virany et al., 1985; Beatty and Zajac, 1985; Grusky, 1963).

Thus, when we consider corporate leadership succession, we see a special aspect of retirement that is not always present for other public figures. This is leaders' responsibility for the continuous well being of their firms. Perhaps we must then appreciate retirement from such offices as more critical than from other occupations. The CEO's challenge is not merely to remain a lively individual contributor. Rather, the challenge is to provide future opportunities for others who are blocked by the leader's mere existence. Personal questions concerning another's age, tenure, and health are not invasions of privacy when the discussion concerns those with substantial control over the destiny of many others. Such discussion on the leader's health and departure have been heightened in public due to the historic records set regarding the ages of national leaders, for example, Ronald Reagan, roughly a decade older than most of his predecessors.

President Woodrow Wilson's later term health distresses are often cited as examples of an unwillingness of a leader to step aside, even when fitness for office was very much in question. Wilson suffered the first of several paralytic strokes on September 25, 1919. For the next 18 months, he was able to function marginally, unable to leave his bedroom, and was far out of contact with most of his subordinates.

This concern over presidential succession was most pronounced after the dynasty of Franklin Delano Roosevelt. Even today, the full range of the political spectrum from liberal democrats to conservative republicans has spoken on the issue, some calling for a six year term of office, others for no limits, and others for the two terms which is the present law. The needs for stability and learning time for a president are balanced by the concerns over the consuming efforts to secure a second term of office, not to mention dangerous consolidations of power (Wicker, 1983). Looking internationally, during Reagan's first term, we witnessed the deaths of four Soviet heads of state, all in their 70s and the resultant confusing handling of international crises during the subsequent power vacuum. The People's Republic of China continued to be led by men in their 80s while other non-communist countries such as the 20-year rule of Ferdinand Marcos in the Phillipines were led by ailing, aged dictators in their 70s or dogmatic despots such as the 85-year-old Ayatollah Khomeini of Iran.

Parallels can be drawn from these extreme examples in politics to the retirement philosophy of leaders in the corporate world. Occidental Petroleum's 87-year-old chief executive Armand Hammer is legendary for his frequent "execution" of probable successors (Business Week, 1984). This alleged "firing squad" style approach to management turnover has been noted in chief executive Harry Grey's reign at United Technologies. His dismissal of President Robert Carlson was followed by unsupported charges of electronic surveillance (Howard, 1984). At Chock-Full-of-Nuts the bedridden octogenarian chief executive had entrusted the daily management of the company to his personal physician, much to the dismay of a large group of shareholders (Bonner, 1982).

The succession story at Puritan Fashions is far more tragic than those above. When 62 year old chief executive Carl Rosen contemplated his retirement from the firm he had run for the last 36 years, he found he had no internal reservoir of senior talent to groom for the top job. Since taking over following his father's death in 1947, Rosen showed a marked inability to retain his senior executive corps. He hired an outside successor, Warren Hirsch, from their leading rival firm. Rosen signed a contract to pay Hirsch over $1 million and announced to the public that the future was in Hirsch's hands. After some sudden reported skirmishes with the company's designer, Calvin Klein, who was also a major shareholder, during the first two months on the job, Hirsch was dismissed with his full $1 million for eight weeks work (for a fuller discussion, see O'Toole, 1984).

Two years after Hirsch's dismissal, Carl Rosen learned that he had cancer and began again to hastily assume the reins given that he had no other successor in mind. More experienced potential heirs had left in frustration with Rosen's "one man show" style. Just before his death, Carl Rosen acknowledged that his son was an unproven, inexperienced successor stating:

> I never really knew him until about four years ago. I was never there when any of the children were born. I was always working.

He sadly confessed:

> I really devoted my life to this company and they paid me well. But as you get older and you put it on the scale of what you gained and what you lost, you wonder if all this was worth it. This industry is tough . . . (Kneale, 1983)

Within a year, this sad story was rounded out by the removal of young Andrew Rosen by disappointed dissident shareholders—again led by Calvin Klein. The thought of succession to Carl Rosen was like suggesting death. When death was imminent, it was too late to groom a successor.

In essence, the chief executive's name becomes figuratively hyphenated with the name of the firm. His or her personal career dreams have become the common property of the firm. Since being selected as the firm's leader, the leader's personal dream has become the guiding organizational vision. When a new leader and a new dream are selected, the departing leader is left with a deflated sense of purpose since his purpose was fulfilled through the mission of the group. When an orchestra conductor retires, it is unlike the retirement of any of the other performers. All the others can leave with their instruments and continue to play solo or in ensembles. But the conductor leaves only with memories, as his instrument, the orchestra, remains behind. In 1960, Eugene Ormandy, music director of the Philadelphia Orchestra said, "The Philadelphia Orchestra sound is me," and music critics resoundingly agreed. He served as music director from 1938 until his reluctant retirement at age 80 in 1980. At this occasion he complained, "One retires when one is dead or ill" (Hughes, 1985). His diminished eyesight, reduced hearing, and heart complications left him no other option beyond withdrawal.

Thus, within his or her own organization, the chief executive has become a folk hero to that immediate community. In making this community contribution through leadership service, chief executives have invested more of their life in their work than most other workers. However, many can become absorbed, dedicated, and even addicted to their work. Chief executives lose personal ownership over their own dream.

As community property, it becomes critiqued, modified, adopted, and ultimately discarded by the organization.

Many heroes do not take well to the destruction of their dreams. Quite often, the heroes within our legends across cultures perform an about face and become villains themselves. For example, recall how King Saul of the Old Testament turned from the grand unifier of the Hebrews to a threatened monarch plotting the death of his likely successor and pro- tege, David. Saul was the first King and although reluctant to lead, he grew attached to adoration of his masses; the growing popularity of his protégé became a threat. The redeemers may become embittered if their plan for salvation is rejected. Those who feel that their goals for the organization have been attained are less likely to resent the setting aside of the dream. Why not discard it if it has been consumed usefully? This article opened with a juxtaposition of those who cling to a position in late career as if one were grasping on for dear life against those who eagerly leave a position late in life, anxious to break free of the role imposed upon them from without. The argument now advanced is that a distinguishing feature between these two clusters of older people is that some people are content with the impact which they have had on others during their careers while some people still seek greater impact.

To some extent, this satisfaction may be determined by the distance which one has traveled in one's life. The resources with which we have been provided related to those which we have developed and utilized help to calibrate our yardstick of success. In the popular film *Cocoon*, aliens from outer space called "antarians" offer retirement community residents at one Florida locale an escape to a land of not only eternal life, but eternal *productive* life. Most eagerly accept this escape from their imminent decaying purposeless existence. A character named Bernie, however, firmly declined the Antarian gift despite the pleading of his friends. At their farewell, he explains that "I was dealt my hand of cards from the start and played as well as I could; it's not fair to want to reshuffle the deck." His senile wife's drifting awareness but constant loving appreciation serves as a reminder of a life filled with little regret. He is grateful and content. As a result, Bernie does not want to relive his life.

Similarly, some leaders want to relive and rework their career if they feel that they did not achieve the truly great heights that were in their grasp. Chief executives, as folk heroes, are driven by more than the desire to use what they have been given. As many of us, they seek to be net contributors rather than net consumers in life. Fifty years ago, psy- choanalytic theorist Otto Rank challenged the sexual basis of doctrinaire Freudian theory to suggest that rather than the pursuit of passion, our lifelong struggle is to conquer the fear of insignificance of life suggested by certainty of death (Rank, 1932; Lieberman, 1985; Becker, 1973). The heroic drive, according to Rank, is the effort to achieve immortality through the heroic legacy, a presumedly lasting imprint upon the society which recognizes the hero. The destruction of the dream is the destruction of the legacy. Heroes, if uncertain of the strength of their contribution, may resemble villains themselves in the defense of their dream of their community. They may become angry at the "selfish" younger generation, the ungrateful society, and the aging process itself, which threatens to erode a lifetime of building.

Recapitulation

In summary, this discussion has introduced three observations about leadership successions and retirement. First, we know very little about the various ways retiring leaders actually leave. Second, the great difficulty of leaving office is underappreciated by society despite its importance. Third, the perpetual scanning of rising generations of leaders deflects attention away from the departing generations of leaders. This lack of balanced understanding of executive entrance and exit aggravates destructive conflict across generations.

Turning to the first general theme we must recognize that some leaders depart office gracefully while others exit like a hurricane. All of our institutions have leaders who must face the ultimate reality of a finite reign. Our literatures on leadership ranging from Machiavelli to current management theorists describe how leaders mobilize and direct their constituents over the course of their reign. The techniques for discharging the responsibilities of office are relayed in academic research journals, best-selling management manuals, and popular magazines. More recent writings also indicate an enhanced appreciation for a more developmental perspective on leadership. This newer literature looks at the rise of new leaders. The emphasis is on the career circumstances surrounding their selection, their grooming, and their taking charge.

We tend to study the transfer of power from the perspective of the person assuming office in all these investigations. We know little about the perspective and circumstances of the person relinquishing power. The emphasis·is upon the rise to the throne and the reign of the ruler. The retirement of the ruler is no less significant to our understanding of the change in command than the rise and the reign. Through this neglect, the retirement event may, in fact, become more critical in explaining succession. Unspoken tensions over how a chief executive leaves office can destroy the continuity of command between predecessors and successors. Political rivalries intensify, tearing the organization apart at the seams, as subordinates align with opposing factions. The tensions can damage the mutual trust and group effectiveness of boards of directors. External parties such as new recruits, financial backers, suppliers, and customers may take a second look at the stability of a firm embroiled in internal succession battles. Most importantly, a loss of clarity of corporate direction may spread through the firm and thus compromise its future well being. On the other hand some leaders may fortify the firm as they leave. We do not know why and when each extreme occurs.

The second major theme of our discussion was that this retirement of the chief executive is not only important and little understood, it is also very difficult. Retirement is a difficult affair for most of us. It is wrong to presume, however, that leaders have an easier time of it than others. It is true that they have access to all sorts of post-retirement resources from bountiful pension plans to wide-ranging business knowledge and to sprawling networks of personal contacts. The dangers of disengagement seem so much more real for those who have less prominence and less money. The loneliness and the poverty of forgotten retirees must not be minimized. Such miseries, however, have been long identified even if not resolved. The massive social security apparatus valiantly tackles the financial woes despite its own inadequate funding and limited coverage for beneficiaries. Newer grass roots efforts of some progressive employers and concerned communities attempt to address the harder issues of social abandonment and waste.

Chief executives, however, face special retirement hardships that have yet to be articulated. The psychological costs of retirement vary across occupations. For many, there are possibilities to replicate some of the lost social conditions of work in retirement settings. This is not easily accomplished for retired leaders. Top leaders, like other prominent figures, have become accustomed to public attention. It may be wearing for some, but the sudden withdrawal of this recognition can be traumatic. Unlike other celebrities, however, chief executives have influence over their constituents. They do not merely play to an audience, they shape it. This mass impact is virtually impossible to recreate in private life. Top leaders only gain this influence by persuading their following that their visions of the future will help to prepare for unknown events. Thus, leader and community share ownership of the dreams. The retirement of a leader often signifies the sudden rejection of the leader's dream. Their career has elevated them to the heights of a local folk hero only to be pushed hastily from these mythic heights. Thus the leader's prominence is as much of a hindrance as a help in accepting retirement.

Lastly, the third major theme of this discussion was that our failure to appreciate retirement as a special hardship for leaders causes us to inadvertently aggravate resentment across generations. Each generation has its own types of career concerns depending on their location in the human life cycle. In early career, we work to gain entry into the adult world. We seek technical expertise, group acceptance, and begin to construct a reputation. In midcareer we examine and question the life structure which we have created. We have become established in some desired ways and trapped in other ways. By late career we are anxious to show that our accumulated wisdom is still deemed beneficial. Our goals include proving our continued contribution. Whether we stay or leave, we are equally concerned about the preservation of our reputation. A company's systematic efforts to locate and promote rising, early career stars make the less mobile midcareer group even more anxious and impatient for the late career group to exit and create space. The late career leaders resent being treated as mere antique equipment left behind from days of past glory. Their legacy may seem especially vulnerable. Some old leaders then muster the power to dig in their heels, determined to again prove their valor once more before being nudged out of office prematurely. Their influence over the firm's destiny and their own succession send cascading waves down the corporate hierarchy. Our limited understanding of the impact of executive retirement patterns, the particular difficulty of leaving top offices, and the growing tension across generations are just cause for people of all ages to be concerned and challenged by retirement.

A graduate from Harvard College, Associate Professor Jeffrey Sonnenfeld has earned M.B.A. and D.B.A. degrees from the Harvard Business School, where he was awarded three special honors: The Academy of Management's Best Dissertation in Social Issues, The Hawthorne Award for Social Research in Industry, *and* The Richard D. Irwin Award for Business Research. *He has taught two second-year M.B.A. courses:* Interpersonal Behavior and Career Management, *and a required first-year course on Human Resource Management. He has served on the editorial boards of the* Academy of Management Journal, Journal of Occupational Behavior, *and the* Academy of Management Executive. *He was also national president of the Careers Division of the Academy of Management. Sonnenfeld's first book,* Corporate Views of the Public Interest, *was published in 1981. His second book is entitled* Managing Career Systems: Channeling the Flow of Executive Careers, *published in 1984. He has written twenty articles including pieces for the* Harvard Business Review, The American Psychologist, Social Forces, Organizational Dynamics *the* Journal of Organizational Behaviour, Human Relations, *the* Academy of Management Journal, *and* Business Horizons. *His research and consulting has been in the areas of corporate social performance and in human resource management. He has worked in human resources at Scott Paper and IBM. Sonnenfeld's current research focuses on mid- and late-career transitions. The mid-career research is presently targeted on middle management retraining in financial service firms. The late-career research is presently focused on the retirement process for chief executives. This has involved research with 200 recently retired chief executives.*

REFERENCES

Barnard, C. I. *The functions of the executive.* Cambridge, MA: Harvard University Press, 1938.

Beatty, R. P., and Zajac, E. J. CEO change and firm performance. *Academy of Management Presentation,* 45th Annual Meeting, San Diego, CA, 1985.

Becker, E. *The denial of death.* NY: The Free Press, 1973.

Bennis, W., and Nanus, B. Leaders: *The strategies for taking charge.* NY: Harper and Row, 1985, pp. 2, 28.

Bernstein, M. The argument against early retirement. *Industrial Relations,* 4(3), 1965.

Bonner, R. Stormy voting session for Chock Full-of-Nuts. *The New York Times,* December 2, 1982, D-1.

Businessweek. Armand Hammer proves he's still king at Oxy. *Businessweek,* September 10, 1984, 41.

Campbell, J. *The hero with a thousand faces.* Princeton, NJ: Princeton University Press, 1949, pp. 18, 30–31.

Churchill, W. C. Address to the House of Commons, June 18, 1940.

Crittendon, J. Aging and party affiliations. *Public Opinion Quarterly,* 1962, **21,** 648–657.

Darby, R. More firms offer early retirement while weighing its pros and cons. *World of Work Report,* 7(8), August 1982, 1.

Donaldson, G., and Lorsch, J. W. *Decision making at the top.* Basic, 1985, pp. 267, 278, 289.

Eistenstadt, S. N. "From generation to generation," *Age groups and social structure.* Glencoe, IL: The Free Press, 1956.

Elden, G. H. Jr. Age differentiation and life course. In A. Inkeles, J. Coleman, and N. Smelser (Eds.), *Review of sociology,* Palo Alto, CA: Stanford, 1973, pp. 165–190.

Erikson, E. H. *Childhood and society,* 2nd ed. NY: Norton, 1963.

Freeman, R. B. *The overeducated American.* NY: Academic Press, 1976.

Freedman, A. M. DuPont surprised as 12,000 employees accept company early retirement offer. *The Wall Street Journal,* April 9, 1985, 6.

Grusky, O. Managerial succession and organizational effectiveness. *American Journal of Sociology,* 1963, **69,** 210–231.

Grusky, O. Managerial succession and organizational effectiveness. In A. Etzioni (Ed.), *A sociological reader in complex organizations,* 2nd Edition, NY: Holt Rinehart Winston, 1969.

Gussow, M. Grit and wit make Ruth Gordon a star. *The New York Times,* September 9, 1985, H-26.

Hall, D. T. *Careers in organization.* Santa Monica, CA: Goodyear, 1976.

Hayes, H. Reflections on turning 80. *Newsweek,* October 20, 1980, 17.

Hambrick, D. C. *The Bankruptcy studies.* Unpublished study, Columbia University, 1985.

Hollie, P. G. Well past age 65, they're still boss. *The New York Times,* July 29, 1979, H-1.

Horowitz, J. *Conversations with Arrau.* NY: Limelight Editions, 1984, 187, 189.

Howard, G. Why Harry Gray can't let go, turmoil at United Technologies. *Fortune,* November 12, 1984, 16–19. See also: Lueck, T. J. Gray still dogged by some charges: Possible heir trained. *The New York Times,* November 30, 1984.

Hughes, A. Eugene Ormandy dead at 85. *The New York Times,* March 23, 1985, A-1, D-23.

Hyman, R. *Political socialization.* Glencoe, IL: The Free Press, 1954.

Jacques, E. Death and the mid-life crisis. *International Journal of Psychoanalysis,* 1965, **46,** 502–514.

Johnson, R. Heineman has a new challenge at Northwest. *The Wall Street Journal,* December 7, 1983, 31.

Johnston, P. D., and Lannaman, R. S. Retired top executives return to work within months of retirement. *News from Russell Reynolds Associates,* press release, December 1984.

Jones, L. Y. *Great expectations: America and the baby boom generation.* NY: Cowot, McCann, Geoghegan, 1980, p. 211.

Jud, R. *The retirement decision: The American managers view their prospects: An AMA survey report.* NY: AMACOM, 1981.

Jung, C. G. *Modern man in search of a soul.* NY: Harcourt Brace, 1933.

Kenisten, K. *Young radicals and notes on committed youth.* NY: Harcourt, Brace, Janovitch, 1976.

Kenisten, K. *Youth and dissent: The rise of a new opposition.* NY: Harcourt, Brace, Janovich, 1971.

Kneale, D. How a third generation came to take control of puritan fashions. *The Wall Street Journal,* September 6, 1983, 1.

Kochan, T. A., and Barucci, T. A. *Human resource management and industrial relations.* Boston, MA: Little Brown, 1985, pp. 231–242.

Kotter, J. *Power and influence.* NY: The Free Press, 1985. (This book discusses the qualities of smooth CEO departures.)

Lawrence, B. L. Age grading: The implicit organizational timetable. In M. B. Arthur and B. L. Lawrence (Eds.), *Environment and career,* Special issue of *The Journal of Occupational Behaviour,* 1985, 5(1).

Lieberman, E. J. *Acts of will: The life and work of Otto Rank.* NY: The Free Press, 1985.

Levinson, D. J., Darrow, C. N., Klein, E. B., Levinson, M. H., and McKee, B. *The seasons of a man's life.* NY: Ballantine, 1978, pp. 35–36.

Levinson, H., and Rosenthal, S. *CEO: Corporate leadership in action.* NY: Basic, 1984, p. 267.

Lubins, J. S., and King, M. L. More employers offer an early retirement: Some workers decline; Firms seek to cut payrolls to open promotion paths. November 12, 1980, 24.

Marquart, P., and McDowell, S. F. *Seniority in the Akison rubber industry.* Wash., D.C.: Bureau of Labor Statistics, 1944, monograph.

Mater, D. A. The development and operations of the railroad seniority system. *Journal of Business,* April 1939, 12, 100.

McConnell, S. Age discrimination in employment. In H. Parnes (Ed.), *Policy issues in work and retirement.* Kalamazoo, MI: Upjohn Institute, 1983, pp. 159–196.

McGinley, L. Mixed signals are baffling forecasters as they try to predict economic growth. *The Wall Street Journal,* August 17, 1985, 21.

Miles, R. E., and Snow, C. C. *Organizational structure, strategy, and process.* NY: McGraw Hill, 1978.

Miller, P. C., and Form, W. H. *Industrial sociology.* NY: Harper, 1951.

National Committee for Manpower Policy. "Discouraged workers, potential workers, and national unemployment policy," Special Report, 1978.

O'Toole, P. *The corporate messiah.* NY: William Morrow, 1984.

Pascale, R. T., and Athens, A. G. *The art of Japanese management.* NY: Simon and Schuster, 1981.

Pelz, D. C., and Andrews, F. M. *Scientists in organizations.* NY: Wiley, 1966.

Perry, J. M. Claude Pepper at 81 delights the elderly, upsets Republicans. *The Wall Street Journal,* August 4, 1982, 1.

Pfeffer, J. "Some consequences of organizational demography: Potential impacts of an aging workforce on formal organizations," presented at the Committee on Aging, National Council, National Academy of Sciences, March 21–23, 1979, Annapolis, MD.

Pyron, H. C., and Greene, H. R. *Pre-retirement counseling, retirement adjustment and the older worker.* Eugene, OR: University of Oregon, 1969.

Rank, O. *Art and artist.* NY: Alfred A. Knopf, 1932, pp. 214–216.

Reich, C. A. *The greening of America.* NY: Random House, 1970.

Ryder, N. B. The whort as a concept in the study of social change. *American Sociological Review,* 1965, 30, 843–861.

Sales and Marketing Management. Jim Ryder has no truck with the old system. *Sales and Marketing Management*, January 12, 1981, 21.

Schein, E. H. How to break in the college graduate. *Harvard Business Review*, November-December 1964, 68–76.

Schein, E. H. The individual, the organization and the career: A conceptual scheme. *Journal of Applied Behavioral Science*, 1971, **7**, 211–217.

76th Congress, 1st Session, Senate Committee on Education and Labor, *Violations of free speech and rights of labor*, Part 45, Wash., D.C.: U. S. Government Printing Office, 1939.

Smith, F. "The push and pull at early retirement." 25th Annual Meetings of the Academy of Management, Detroit, MI, 1980.

Sonnenfeld, J. Dealing with an aging workforce. *Harvard Business Review*, November–December 1978, **56**(6), 81–92.

Turner, W. Eric Hoffer—Dock worker–author who looked into life, dies at 80. *The New York Times*, May 22, 1983, 34.

U. S. Bureau of the Census. Estimates and projections of the population 1977–2050. *Current population reports*, Series p. 25, No. 704, July 1977.

Vaillant, G. E. *Adaptations to life*. Boston, MA: Little Brown, 1977.

Virany, B., Tushman, M. L., and Romanell, E. A longitudinal study of the determinants and effects of executive succession. *Academy of Management Presentation*, 45th Annual Meeting, San Diego, CA, 1985.

Wagner, W. C., Pfeffer, J., and O'Reilly, C. A. Organizational demography and turnover in top management groups. *Administration Sciences Quarterly*, 1984, **29**, 74–92.

Weber, M. *The theory of social economic organization*, translated by T. Parsons. NY: Oxford University Press, 1947.

Wechsberg, J. *The merchant bankers*. NY: Simon and Schuster, 1966, pp. 176–177.

Wermiel, S. Top court is to rule on seniority issue in voluntary affirmative actions plans. *The Wall Street Journal*, April 16, 1985, 8.

White, R. W. Motivation reconsidered: The concept of competence. *The Psychological Review*, Sept. 1959, **66**.

Wicker, T. Six years for presidency? *The New York Times Magazine*, June 26, 1983, 16–19, 52–58.

Human Resource Management In Action

On Executive Succession: A Conversation with Lester B. Korn

Douglas M. Cowherd*

Many organizations are undertaking major strategic reorientations in response to the worldwide turbulence of the 1970s and 1980s. Experience has shown that the successful pursuit of these new strategic directions requires executives with skills that match the strategies. However, in many cases these skills are not possessed by an organization's existing management team, and the search for leadership turns to outsiders. As a result, there has been an enormous increase in the movement of executives between companies and in the use of executive search firms to find and recruit outside talent. Revenues of the two largest executive recruiting firms have increased over 130% in the last five years.

The business of executive recruiting has not always been so dynamic. Executive search was a no-growth industry before 1970, and recruiting practices were far less sophisticated than those of today's leading firms. As there were no requirements for special educational degrees or professional certification, and little need for capital investment, there were few barriers to entering the search business. Virtually anyone with an office and a telephone could hang up a shingle and begin to conduct searchers. Consequently, much of the search work was done by small firms that consisted of a few partners and a minimal support staff. Search consultants were generally over 50 years old, and had left previous jobs

* The author would like to thank Alan Lafley and Windle Priem for providing insights on the nature of the executive recruiting business. Carole Barnett, Stew Friedman, and Michelle Kaminski made many helpful editorial comments.

in industry. They formed a tight old-school-tie network, largely based on the east coast, in which aggressive competition for business was frowned on. The primary role of the executive recruiter was to act as the client's agent in handling the delicate matter of contacting possible job candidates.

The situation in the executive recruiting industry began to change in the late 1960s. A major factor in changing the nature of the industry was the entry of Korn/Ferry International. Lester Korn and Dick Ferry met in 1962 while working in Los Angeles for the accounting firm Peat, Marwick, Mitchell. Subsequent to becoming partners of the firm, Korn and Ferry left in 1969 to establish their own executive search company, which would bring the practices and standards of professional service firms, such as management consulting and accounting, into the search business.

Korn/Ferry innovated in three domains. First, the firm created specialty practice groups that focused on recruiting in particular industries. Second, Korn/Ferry developed a computerized database containing background data on possible job candidates. This allowed consultants in the entire Korn/Ferry network to scan an extensive pool of management talent with relative ease and speed. Third, Korn/Ferry established a global network of offices. Korn/Ferry began its global expansion in 1972 by moving into Europe, and established Tokyo's first executive search office in 1973. In following years the company extended its recruiting network to Asia, Australia, Canada, Mexico, and South America. Korn/Ferry now has 37 offices in 15 countries, and its client list numbers 1250 organizations, among them many of the world's largest industrial and financial powers.

Clients appreciated the Korn/Ferry approach, for it provided them with the level of professionalism and service they had come to demand from other consulting firms. Korn/Ferry revenues shot up accordingly. Korn/Ferry is now the biggest search firm, with 1985 worldwide revenues of approximately $60 million. While many firms in the executive recruiting business are developing sophisticated practices that parallel those of Korn/Ferry, the firm has ruffled some feathers in the industry. Competitors claim that Korn/Ferry has been overly aggressive in a business that has always been characterized by tact and discretion. However, these complaints may be due to the disruption of the traditional order in an insular, east coast based industry caused by the successful incursion of two innovative young men from Southern California.

Lester Korn's position as Chairman and CEO of Korn/Ferry provides him with a unique window on executive succession and the development of the recruiting business. In this candid interview, Korn comments on the inability of many companies to operate effective succession systems for upper echelon managers, at a time when corporate boards are increasingly requiring top management to show that good succession plans are in place. Korn believes that companies should look to search firms for ongoing assistance in executive assessment and succession planning, rather than waiting until critical problems arise in the executive ranks. Further, Korn discusses the roles that should be played by the executive search firm and a company's human resource function as they collaborate in dealing with executive succession. Finally, Korn speculates that in the future the executive search industry will be dominated by a few large firms that will provide their clients with a greater range of more sophisticated services.

COWHERD: As an experienced executive recruiter, you are in a unique position to observe the operation of succession systems in a wide variety of organizations. How effective are these systems?

KORN: They are not particularly good. The succession process is pretty effective at the middle management level because you can quantify the managerial characteristics that are required. And thought is given to things like merit reviews, progress reports, and the meeting of objectives, particularly in larger corporations. However, as you move into the top five to twenty positions—depending on the size of the company—you find that longevity, luck, and just being in the right place at the right time have been far too important in getting people into their positions. This isn't a fatal problem, because it can be corrected. I think that in the last five to ten years the larger corporations, particularly in certain industries like banking, have worked hard on the succession of top executives. General Electric is a good example of a company with a very progressive approach. This means knowing the roles you want executives to play and defining them properly. Then you must have a training system in place so executives can develop in the right direction. For example, people could be given international experience early in their careers if that is an important element of what they may be doing in future roles. I think companies are getting better at this sort of thing. However, while many people talk about succession planning, so far there have been few positive results, to the detriment of companies and shareholders. While there are noteworthy exceptions, in most companies it usually takes a crisis to trigger serious succession efforts.

COWHERD: What prevents companies from managing succession in the top echelon as well as they do in middle management?

KORN: Part of the problem is that the human resource executive who understands succession issues is usually not part of the key management group. The other problem is that top executives tend to get very defensive about succession. With limited access at the level where the decisions are made, the human resource people can only watch and wait. The good news is that corporate board members are getting increasingly involved in management succession issues and are forcing top managers to deal with them. Directors are saying they want to know about plans for developing the talent needed to replace key executives, and they want to see tangible results.

COWHERD: So boards are beginning to look at succession plans in the same light as financial plans. They want to know that both are in place.

KORN: That's right. Our annual board study backs this up. We ask the board chairmen of the Fortune 1000 companies to rate the importance of the issues that their companies will be facing five years from now. Directors rate succession planning as the third most important issue, behind only financial results and strategic planning.

COWHERD: Senior executives tend to jealously guard their freedom to act without board interference. Can boards play an active role in succession without hampering management?

KORN: Succession planning is not the responsibility of management alone. The board has to protect the balance sheet of the corporation for the shareholders, and has the same obligation to protect the human resource asset base for the shareholders. And they're much better at protecting the financial assets than they are at protecting the human resources.

COWHERD: Many boards have defined their role in executive succession as limited to dealing with CEO succession, with the CEO being responsible for succession at lower levels. You're saying that if directors are serious about maintaining high quality management they will have to get involved with succession farther down into the executive ranks.

KORN: Boards have to deal with the top five to seven executive positions. At the very least, they need to be aware of the plans that exist for these slots. However, I'm not saying that they should substitute their judgement for that of the CEO. They just need to make sure that somebody is doing a thorough job of assessing people and planning for the future.

COWHERD: What role do you think the human resource executive should take in the succession process?

KORN: Selecting and developing executive talent for succession is the line manager's responsibility, but human resource managers need to play a more active and constructive role in improving the succession process. The success of their efforts depends on the strong support of top management. Fortunately, human resource executives are now starting to get the recognition they deserve. Increasingly, they are involved in the strategic planning process, and are asked by the CEO to take primary responsibility for developing an implementation plan to ensure the availability of the critical human resources needed in the strategy-driven succession plan.

COWHERD: What systems and practices should the human resource manager try to put in place in order to accomplish this?

KORN: There are a few things that should be standard operating procedure. Heading the list are effective management resources review sessions that are conducted on a continuous basis at all management levels, and a disciplined candidate review and selection process to fill key positions when openings occur. The management resources review process must identify outstanding individuals and plan for their development. Where the process is working well, top managers make sure that the development plans are being implemented according to well-defined schedules. Human resource executives should add value by designing and managing the process, but the selection decisions should remain the responsibility of line managers. I know many CEOs and top managers who are looking to their human resource managers for this kind of help in making significant improvements in the overall quality of management in their companies.

COWHERD: Do you think that the role of the human resource manager in facilitating the succession process requires a structural division of the human resource function?

KORN: Of course it's advantageous to keep the human resource function tightly integrated. However, if management resources planning and development is not getting the attention it deserves, it may be a good idea to separate this work from other human resource activities. I think you're going to see more separation of management planning because it is a critical function and requires very different expertise from the more traditional personnel activities. For the senior human resource person to give sufficient attention to succession, someone else must be managing the more routine personnel activities on a day-to-day basis. Otherwise the management resources planning and development work won't get done.

COWHERD: You are describing a wider range of human resource department activity than is common in many organizations. Do senior human resource managers have the skills and background that are required for them to take a leading role in dealing with management succession?

KORN: Some do, but many don't. This role is relatively new, and to date the human resource function has been slow to fill it. There are still too few human resource people who are both capable of doing good management resources planning and development, and are allowed to do it. And this is no easy task. To ensure strong management, human resource people have got to design, implement, and manage an integrated system. They have got to deal with college recruiting for entry-level positions, early identification of promising individuals, development of the most talented people, and an effective executive succession process. It's the total system that's important. All of the components must mesh, and this requires both skill and some trial and error experience.

COWHERD: What are some of the typical mistakes made by human resource managers who are initiating a more sophisticated succession process?

KORN: They tend to put too much focus on the mechanics of succession planning and too little on research-based management resource planning and development. Some people spend a great deal of time on color coding the boxes on organization charts, and generating a list of people who could move into those boxes. The focus ought to be on good assessment—using solid performance data—of individuals from a broad talent pool. Human resource people need as much hard data as possible on the people identified as future managers and leaders. They will do much better in identifying candidates—both internal and external—if they focus on establishing a disciplined selection and identification process, and on individual development planning, than if they continue to focus on the mechanics of succession planning. Succession planning is essential, but even the term itself tends to lead to an overemphasis on the mechanics at the expense of the critical elements of the process.

COWHERD: I'd like to move our discussion from the internal corporate succession system to the role of the executive search firm. You have pioneered many of the practices that are now standard operating procedure in the executive search business. In light of your comments on what companies should be doing for themselves, what is the best role for external search firms—how can search firms be most helpful to their clients?

KORN: In Fortune 1000 companies, about 80 percent of the successors to top executive jobs come from within a company. Twenty percent come from outside. Companies sometimes think it's a sign of weakness to go outside, but that's not the case at all. Some companies look at outside candidates simply to ensure that the internal candidate is the best candidate. But circumstances can change. Companies grow rapidly, or they fail to groom the right people. Occasionally they decide that they're too inbred and they want to go outside to inject fresh thinking. Sometimes a crisis occurs and there is no one inside the company who can handle it. So there are a number of reasons for bringing in an executive search firm. The appropriate roles for the search firm range from helping to evaluate the existing crop of contenders, to determining what kind of talent is available outside the company, to helping them refine what it is they should be looking for. Then the role of the executive search firm is to locate, evaluate, and attract competent candidates, then present them to the client for review. Implicit in all of this are detailed job descriptions, performance goals, and selection criteria, which we sometimes help to establish.

COWHERD: After the client decides who they want, there is still the sensitive stage of closing the deal. To what extent should the search consultant become involved in the negotiations over compensation and other terms of employment?

KORN: That's essential. The job is not done until the candidate is landed. Identifying the best person for a job is critical, but convincing someone to make the move is often the most difficult part of the process.

COWHERD: What does it take to fill a CEO position in a major corporation?

KORN: The population of people with the ability to be a CEO or COO is very limited. For any given job, there are probably only 20 to 25 truly qualified candidates who have had the right experience in a line position with profit and loss responsibility, the proper interpersonal and communication skills, and the kind of background that matches the corporation's needs for the next five to ten years. The person has to have the right chemistry to work with the board and has to fit into the corporate culture. Our task is to prioritize these items, find the person who best fits the criteria, and then continue the matchmaking to a successful conclusion. It's our job to help the client understand what it takes to attract a top flight job candidate, and to help the candidate understand the potential benefits of making a career move.

COWHERD: You are arguing that search firms should take on a much broader role than they typically do, including redefining jobs and assessing in-house candidates. These are often considered to be internal matters that should be handled by the human resource function. How deeply should a search firm delve into their client's affairs?

KORN: One of the questions that search firm partners must ask when they are engaged in a senior level assignment is "Why isn't there an internal candidate?" You cannot do a good search if you don't understand this. Sometimes the reasons are very simple. A new division may have just been created, or a merger has occurred. Sometimes a company unexpectedly loses the head of a division, and so no successor had been groomed. When a company clarifies its long range plan some executives may not have what it takes to meet the goals. Other times there is an aging problem. I know one multibillion dollar corporation that's wrestling with this problem right now. The CEO is 62 and the COO is 63 and the next two or three people are in their early sixties or late fifties. This company is rich in talent, but the age distribution is wrong. There is no group of able people who are ten years younger. Below this very senior group are a bunch of young turks running the divisions. The current top management is going to have to make a difficult decision between picking one of those young turks or bringing in a new president from outside. The search firm needs to have a good understanding of the internal condition of the company in order to provide the best service to the company.

COWHERD: How should an executive search firm and the client company's human resource function work together?

KORN: A search firm can be a valuable consulting resource for the human resource function. Human resource departments call in search firms because they have access to a wider network of staffing sources than those readily available to any single client. Furthermore, a search firm is geared up to carry out a search in a more timely and efficient manner. But the human resource executive and the search consultants should work together in a close client–professional relationship and avoid the trap of competing with each other. First, they need to work together to develop the position specification. The corporate human resource person should have the best knowledge of what the organization needs, but the consultant brings to the search a great deal of experience in finding individuals for similar jobs. And it is easier for the search consultant to define the corporate culture objectively than it is for the client, because the client is part of it. Frequent communication between the two helps the search to proceed faster and more smoothly. The result is that weak candidates can be eliminated more quickly.

COWHERD: What is an inappropriate role for a search firm?

KORN: I think you can use search firms for jobs that are too small. Korn/Ferry doesn't like to take on searches under the $75,000 to $100,000 base salary range. It's just not cost effective. Another problem occurs when the search firm can't provide consultants who are familiar with the client's business. Last week I was approached by a client who wanted me to do a search for him. He is looking for someone who understands how to create products and expand the markets for nonmetalic chemical products. I'm absolutely the wrong person for that search because I don't know the first thing about the business. However, one of my partners has worked in this area a dozen times and he knows exactly what the client is talking about. He's the right one for the assignment. I'm an awfully good search person but if I don't understand the technology of the company, no matter how good I am, I shouldn't be handling a search. Consequently, the large search firms, spurred by Korn/Ferry, have moved towards specialization. For instance, we have specialists in real estate, banking, health care, and not-for-profit institutions. Our 120 partners are divided between specialty divisions and general practice, but virtually each of them has a personal specialty. Specialization is something that we pioneered, and it's one place where the big firms have an advantage.

COWHERD: The top management echelon is a very political environment and nothing is more politically charged than succession. Have you ever found yourself involved in a search that was really a charade that was taking place for political reasons?

KORN: Not really, we're too expensive for that. Search firms try to avoid taking assignments unless the client really has a job description and knows where they're going with that position. We don't want to fail. We don't want to take the client's money and spend three or four months talking to scores of people only to have the client claim that we haven't come up with anyone. That's not good for us and its not good for them. Sure, some searches are cancelled because a client decides not to go forward or they decide to promote from within, but my firm has a very high fulfillment rate. I'm sure my competitors have the same rate. Searches are not being started frivolously, particularly for senior level positions. It's too expensive and too disruptive for a corporation to do so.

COWHERD: The executive search business has grown quite rapidly in the last ten years, and practices have changed substantially. In many ways, Korn/Ferry has been at the forefront of the changes. What direction do you see Korn/Ferry and its competitors taking in the next ten years?

KORN: I think Korn/Ferry will be much larger. New specialty divisions will be created and more international offices opened. Korn/Ferry will go much further with its concept of client partners. For example, we do work for Nissan Motors in many parts of the world. In fact, we brought in Marvin Runyon to head their operations in the United States. All of our work for Nissan is managed by a partner in our Tokyo office. Also, I have a partner in charge of Europe who handles work for many of our European clients that have American operations. As you know, many of the major international companies are now investing heavily in American businesses. I foresee increasingly close relationships between Korn/Ferry client partners and their clients, which should lead to increased business for us. This could be much like the relationship between a senior partner in a law firm and the CEO of the company that has the firm on retainer.

COWHERD: As part of an attempt to establish a deeper connection with the client, will you move to an annual retainer basis for charging your clients, rather than a fee basis?

KORN: Interestingly enough, for a short time after we founded Korn/Ferry we charged an annual retainer fee, unlike everybody else in the industry. However, I don't see a retainer-based service in the near future, although I do see higher fees being established. For the last ten years fees have been at one-third of the first year salary for the job. Another future trend will be greater research sophistication in the search firms. Korn/Ferry has poured millions of dollars into data processing systems and research. Our database on potential job candidates is second to none. We have to be able to do good research or else we're not going to find the right people. I also think one of the things we have to concern ourselves about is potential governmental regulation. We have to be very mindful of government regulations dealing with discrimination and fair employment practices.

COWHERD: Right now there are a few big firms, such as Korn/Ferry, Heidrick and Struggles, and Russell Reynolds, and a large number of small outfits, many specializing in a single industry or geographic region. What do you think will happen to the structure of the executive search industry in the future?

KORN: I think we will see more concentration in the industry. There will be four to six major search firms worldwide, in much the same structure as the big eight accounting firms. The firms will have mutually exclusive client relationships, which is not the way it is today. Currently, the Fortune 500 companies tend to let each of their divisions choose the search firms they want to work with. In our last survey we found that the average large corporation had engaged five search firms, somewhere in the organization. That isn't a very effective use of search firms. I remember a few years ago I met with the executive vice president of a major food-oriented conglomerate who said that he wanted his company to become more important to us as a client so that they would get more attention. I think that this is the path of the future. Now they're getting better service because we have a partner who spends almost all of his time in directing our worldwide work for this client.

COWHERD: Will Korn/Ferry expand into providing what has traditionally been viewed as management consulting services, such as organizational restructuring and compensation studies?

KORN: I don't think we'll be competing with consulting firms like McKinsey or Booz, Allen and Hamilton. However, our people have to get a better understanding of management issues that are broader than pure executive recruiting. For example, we have to have extensive knowledge of compensation schemes. We don't have a single client that doesn't ask about the appropriate salary range for a job, and how to put together the right compensation package. And job candidates always ask us how much money they should ask for. We are already providing both organizational and compensation services, and I believe that we may charge an add-on fee for this kind of work, at some point in time. However, I don't see us installing a complete compensation program for a major corporation. But as part of doing good search work we've got to do some sophisticated compensation and organization planning.

COWHERD: When you talk about doing this kind of work, you're suggesting a role for the search firm that is much broader than the common conception. The role would be extended to include working with clients to ensure that managerial talent is developed internally whenever possible, and to advising on the proper organizational structure and compensation practices to support the executives who are in place. Rather than concentrating entirely on recruiting, there would also be some attention paid to motivating and retaining key executives. Succession would still be the central focus, but the sophisticated search firm would approach the issue from multiple directions.

KORN: That's right. I think that succession planning will get better and that search firms will enter the succession planning process at an earlier stage. Companies will show more foresight, instead of waiting to take action until a position has been vacant for six months and the situation has reached the crisis level. They will recognize, for example, that they really don't have anyone lined up for a position where a successor will be needed in three years, and that they had better do something about it now. They will understand that going outside the firm for a replacement is only one of the options.

COWHERD: So Korn/Ferry might get involved in such things as management development and planning career paths for key executives?

KORN: The more sophisticated partners of this firm are already doing this with their clients.

COWHERD: That's an interesting view of the future. It would be a big transition from the days when surreptitious recruiters hid behind potted plants in the lobby and whispered to prospects "Hey buddy, have I got a job for you!"

KORN: That's why we've got that big potted plant here in this meeting room. That thing is going to die as the symbol of the search profession. The best search firms are becoming very sophisticated in working with their clients to develop top management teams that can lead a company to peak performance.

Douglas Cowherd is OASIS (Organization and Strategy Information Service) Program Manager with The Hay Group, and a doctoral student in Organizational Psychology at the University of Michigan. His current research deals with the impact of organizational culture on business performance, and the relationship between managerial characteristics and success in strategy implementation.

CPSIA information can be obtained at www.ICGtesting.com
Printed in the USA
LVOW07s0018191015

458792LV00016B/215/P